American Country Christmas

1989

COMPILED & EDITED BY
PATRICIA DREAME WILSON
SUSAN RAMEY WRIGHT

Oxmoor
House®

© 1989 by Oxmoor House, Inc.
Book Division of Southern Progress Corporation
P.O. Box 832463, Birmingham, Alabama 35201

Library of Congress Catalog Number: 89-61909
ISBN: 0-8487-0773-7
ISSN: 1044-4904
Manufactured in the United States of America
First Printing

Executive Editor: Nancy J. Fitzpatrick
Production Manager: Jerry Higdon
Associate Production Manager: Rick Litton
Art Director: Bob Nance

American Country Christmas 1989

Editor: Patricia Dreame Wilson
Assistant Editor: Susan Ramey Wright
Contributing Editor: Charlotte Hagood
Senior Designer: Cynthia R. Cooper
Copy Chief: Mary Jean Haddin
Editorial Assistant: Susan Smith Cheatham
Production Assistant: Theresa L. Beste
Artists: Barbara Ball, Rick Tucker

Assistant Foods Editor: Laura N. Massey
Test Kitchen Director: Julie Fisher
Test Kitchen Home Economists: Nancy C. Earhart,
    Christina A. Pieroni, Gayle Hays Sadler, Paula N.
    Saunders, Jill Wills
Editorial Assistants: Pam Beasley Bullock, Pamela
    Whyte

To find out how you can order *Cooking Light* magazine, write to *Cooking Light*®, P.O.Box C-549, Birmingham, AL 35283

Contents

Introduction 1

Country Christmas at Home

A Bit of New England in Texas 4
Entwine Your Home in Grapevine Charm . . . 10
Making Friends with Herbs 12
Welcome to a Country Yuletide Feast 16
All Through the House 22
Santa Fe Wreaths 25
Ideas: Celebrate with Miniwreaths 28

A Country Christmas Pantry

Serve Up Some Sweet Delights 32
Sugar 'n Spice and Gingerbread's Nice 35
Country Market Gift Ideas 36
Tabletops from the Pantry 39
Quick and Easy—but Oh, So Good! 42
A Friendship Apron to Stencil 47
A Calico Bear with Candy Treats 48
Ideas: Festive Trims for Tasty Fare 50

Treasured Traditions

Deck Your Halls with Sunday Toys 54
Home-Baked Traditions 58
Simple Sheep with an Old-World Appeal 63
The Landscape of Christmas 64
Start a Star-Bright Tradition 66

A Father's Christmas Legacy 70
Hearty Northwest Christmas Breakfast 72
Folk Art Ornaments 75
A Tradition of Friendship 76
Ideas: Handed Down with Love 78

Holiday Handiwork

Bitty Bears 82
A Needlecrafter's Christmas 83
Classic Country Cousins 88
Connecticut Craftsmen 90
Put a Little Punch in Your Christmas 95
Craft-Inspired Cookies 97
Cookie-Mold Ornaments 104
Country Sheep to Cuddle 106
Santa Bear Is Coming to Town! 107
Shadow-Quilted Cards 108
Ideas: These Paper Crafts Are Child's Play . . 110

Pleasures of the Season

A Ho-Ho-Happy Birthday 114
Fireside Cheer .118
Christmas at a Country Inn 123
Wow! A Kitchen Party for Kids! 125
Letters to Santa 129
Cozy Sweatshirts for Christmas Fun 130
Ideas: Holiday for the Birds 132

Patterns 134
Contributors 154
Index 155

emember the Christmas stockings your mother made? They hung in a special spot on the mantel, waiting for a visit from a certain jolly old elf. The tree was aglow with handmade ornaments. The scent of evergreen mixed with aromas from the kitchen as Grandmother put the final touches on mouth-watering sweets you'd dreamed of for so long.

Memories like these greet each of us as we anticipate Christmas. Every year we seek to create for ourselves and our families a holiday season worthy of our dearest childhood memories—an old-fashioned Christmas.

With this premier edition of *American Country Christmas*, we hope you'll be inspired to create just such a special holiday—one from which lasting memories will be made. We give you country decorating tips from Christmas past. We offer easy patterns and instructions for priceless handmade gifts and recipes for holiday fare that your family and friends will long remember. We tell stories of folks all over America who have a talent for celebrating Christmas with a country flair.

Pour a cup of hot cider, curl up in a comfortable chair, and travel with us to a long-ago time when Christmas was a matter of the heart and home.

Patricia D. Wilson

Susan R. Wright

Country Christmas at Home

A BIT OF NEW ENGLAND
IN A TEXAS CHRISTMAS

WELCOME TO A
COUNTRY YULETIDE FEAST

ALL THROUGH THE HOUSE

SANTA FE WREATHS

IDEAS: CELEBRATE THE
SEASON WITH
MINIWREATHS

A Bit of New England in a Texas Christmas

"I always try to decorate with the natural materials that our ancestors would have had on hand," Joan says. "Things like fruits and nuts and popcorn."

Joan Lee knows how to give kids a good time at Christmas. When her three sons were young, they would invite friends over to decorate gingerbread men. Joan would spread out every known candy sprinkle and colored icing and then let the boys have free rein in her kitchen. She would bake batch after batch of little brown men to keep up with the boy artists.

The boys are young men now, no longer interested in decorating cookies, but still available for some old-fashioned Christmas cheer. When they look around their parents' New England saltbox-style home, they are sure to find remembrances of Christmas past.

"My favorite Christmas decorations are the things the boys made when they were really young," Joan says. "They used to give me pictures of themselves taken with Santa every year. They knew it was my dearest gift. I've framed them, and now I put them up as decorations in their bedrooms each holiday."

An abundance of garlands made from cranberries, nuts, and apple slices also adds a festive touch. "I always try to decorate with the natural materials that our ancestors would have had on hand," Joan says. "Things like fruits and nuts and popcorn." This keeps the decorating simple, and in a house with this much character, the less decoration the better.

Fifteen years ago when Joan and her husband, Jack, were building their home, it was a challenge to find 18th- and 19th-century building materials, such as square nails and string latches. That was before the Bicentennial and Mary Emmerling's book, *American Country,* reacquainted people with country style. But probably the biggest challenge of all lay in the location of the New England saltbox—Houston, Texas.

"There were few mail-order sources then," Joan remembers. "And very few people in Houston were acquainted with the style I was striving for. People today have so many more

Left: Every detail of this house is true to the period, including the custom-scored door. This and all the doors were made on site.

The six-foot Christmas tree was landed by Joan at a silent-bid auction at a Christmas homes tour. She wraps the cone-and-pod tree in plastic for storage and then uses a hair dryer to get the dust off when it's time to unpack. The punched-tin star was made by a friend's husband, and the banner was a gift from Joan's sister.

Opposite: Members of the Lee family relax in their kitchen, to string just one more garland of cranberries and to have a nice chat. Left to right: Joan, Scott, Jack, Randy, Misty, and Jacky.

"Out here the style is 'the bigger the better'; our lean style must have seemed very strange to the contractor," says Joan.

advantages with all the magazines, books, and mail-order catalogs."

Joan is an admitted perfectionist. She "lived" in her house for four years before it was built. "I walked around with this house in my head. I knew where every electric plug would be and which way every door would open," she says. Basing her knowledge on a home-management class at the University of Cincinnati, Joan drew the floor plans for their home. She knew she wanted simple, square rooms to use as a backdrop for her antique furnishings.

Long before the ground was broken, wheels were in motion to furnish the house with pieces from the period between 1750 and 1850. The authentic style extended from corner cupboards to candlesticks. Acquiring the pieces took more than the usual wheeling and dealing, but every summer Joan had time for some serious antiquing when Jack's job as a professional quarterback took him away from home.

"When Jack was away at training camp for nine weeks every summer, I knew I could get away with murder, because he'd be so happy to see us when he got home," Joan says. She spent the time selling off recliners and replacing them with leather wing chairs. "One time I had sold our Italian provincial bedroom set. I was hauling furniture down the hall when Jack called to say he'd be home in five minutes for a surprise weekend visit. He caught me red-handed that time," Joan says, with a laugh.

Now Misty, oldest son Jacky's new bride, is hooked on country style, too. She and Joan hit the yard sales and flea markets every chance they get. Maybe one old-fashioned Christmas in the future, Jacky and Misty will have just such tales to tell.

Above left: During the holidays the meat-drying rack over the fireplace doubles as a garland rack. When not draped in garlands, the rack holds decorative utensils.

Left: This folding bed from New England, in the corner, comes in handy for long naps on weekends. Made of tiger-striped maple, it has three sets of legs so that it can be folded up against the wall when not in use. The privacy curtains are made from antique monogrammed bed linens.

Above: A cat the size of Cheekie sleeps wherever she wants, and she's chosen a choice spot by the fire in the Lees' keeping room. Also waiting by the fire is a collection of stockings. The red stocking bears a glittery name on top—Joan. It was her stocking when she was a little girl. Her mom knit the gray and the green argyle socks for Joan's dad many years ago, so Joan now uses them as Christmas stockings for her parents when they come to visit. The goose wears a red knitted hat this year, but every year there's a difference. "Sometimes I put hats on all my decoys; sometimes they get winter scarves," Joan says.

Left: In Jacky's room upstairs stands a group of Christmas trees Joan has collected over the years. Her mom made the ceramic one on the left. A friend made the tree of seed pods and nuts.

The green iron elephant is a bookmark; the red iron dog, a pencil holder.

Below: A Pennsylvania sawbuck table and yoke-back banister chairs set the style for this warm and inviting dining room. The Windsor knuckle armchair was made about 1780.

"This year I had a hankering for orange," Joan says in defense of her persimmons, kumquats, and oranges for Christmas color.

Above: These two headboards were once the head and foot of a single four-poster hickory bed. Joan did the wall stenciling, using a Janet Waring design. "It always looks great at Christmas," she says. The planning, spacing, and stenciling took her several weeks to complete.

The blue-and-white quilted bear was made by a friend 20 years ago. Joan bought it at a yard sale a few years back, not knowing who had made it until her friend came by to visit and said, "I made that bear!"

Right: One year Joan's mom made decorations from glass eggs, adding pictures of the Lee boys when they were little. Now the ornaments find a home every year on the old feather tree in the guest bedroom. The tree also sports a chenille garland from the thirties, antique icicles, and white carrot shapes coated with mica. Joan found the beads at a garage sale and decided to use them on the tree, "just to introduce some blue."

Entwine Your Home in Grapevine Charm

Turn your home into a holiday gallery of grapevine art. Wild grapevine is easy to work with. And it can be found in abundance in woodlands throughout the United States.

Grapevine can be cut and used at any time of the year; but autumn is the ideal time—after the leaves have fallen off and the vine is turning brown, but while it is still pliable. An overnight soak in water will make the vines even more manageable.

If you've never worked with grapevine, you may prefer to start with a simple wreath. But don't stop there. Once you've got a feel for the material, be adventurous. Take a look at the examples on these pages. You may want to duplicate them. Or perhaps you'll be inspired to strike off in new directions to create your own rustic grapevine art.

Below: David Hill's jolly grapevine reindeer seems almost to move before your eyes. To make him, David first created a wire form suggesting the animal's shape. Then he wrapped the form with grapevines and added a sprangly limb for antlers. A red-and-black plaid muffler and an ivy garland dress up the reindeer for the holidays.

Above: David Hill of Birmingham, Alabama, combined rustic grapevine with artificial greenery for his country Christmas tree. He cut a large purchased grapevine wreath in half, separated the vines, and wrapped the curved sections around the front half of the tree. Lengths of natural-colored paper twist and strands of nuts follow the spiral of grapevines on David's tree. Handmade ornaments and dried German statice, nestled in every crevice, make the tree a study in country splendor.

Left: When Robin Medsker was asked to decorate a house on a tour for the Historic Foundation in Fredericksburg, Virginia, she encountered a challenge—the owner of the house was allergic to evergreens. So, Robin and her mother created this man-high grapevine tree, decorated with tiny white lights and a spiral of dried flowers. Robin also made the pinecone bear on the pie safe and the pinecone bunny on the floor.

Above: Robin first tied straight saplings together to form a teepee the height that she wanted her tree to be. Next, using bunches of grapevine, a handful thick and five to six feet long, she wrapped the tree frame, securing the vines with twine. For the small section at the top of the tree, Robin recommends using very young vines and soaking them in warm water.

11

Making Friends with Herbs

*A clear brook runs beneath a low stone bridge at the
edge of the woods. A little girl sits to one side, admiring her
garden. A tangle of mint, thyme, oregano, sage, dill,
and chives hugs each side of the stream. After a moment the girl
heads for the woods with a small trowel in one hand, a basket in
the other. She comes back with wildflowers—a basketful of
forget-me-nots and lilies of the valley, ready for planting.*

Marion Bates remembers those happy childhood days, when her mother gave her a few leftover herb plants from the main garden. That childhood fun time turned into a lifetime love.

"It was truly fanciful," Marion remembers. "I had a bug and bird cemetery in one corner of the garden. And there were flowers, like geraniums, marigolds, and petunias, mixed in with the herbs; but there was no great plan. I guess it was a real country garden."

Marion is still a natural gardener today. A tour around her winter garden in Reading, Pennsylvania, however, shows that a plan does exist. Thyme, lavender, winter savory, and other woody-stem plants flank paths and borders, even in December.

Marion shares her secret for a healthy garden. "Mulch, mulch, mulch. It keeps the weeds out," Marion says simply. She also adds wood chips and mushroom soil, which comes from the mushroom farms in nearby Chester County.

When you walk into her home on a winter afternoon, many scents rise to greet you. The aroma of fresh-squeezed cider mingles with potpourri of dried rosebuds, spruce, cinnamon, cedar, and lavender. You'll probably have a mug of cider; but if you're not in the mood for that, there's always a refreshing concoction of Marion's Thirteen Mint tea. The cider's made from apples picked in her front yard; the mints grow in her formal herb garden.

Marion's love of herbs extends to the name she has given a small house in back—The Herb Haus. "This was the original family house, probably built in 1740," Marion explains. "The first family to live here was German, so my husband, David, and I gave the little house a German name." Once in The Herb Haus you are taken aback by its simplicity. In the middle of the

small room, a table is filled with arrangements and wreaths near completion. Late-afternoon winter light pours in through one window. And up in the loft, almost 300 cheese boxes are neatly stacked and filled with dried herbs.

Marion's home garden supplies her with all the herbs she uses throughout the year. She has put together twelve different herb lectures over the years. She speaks to national conventions around the country about the historical, biblical, and horticultural uses of herbs. She also discusses the use of herbs for cooking and dyeing.

"My first lecture I entitled 'Making Friends with Herbs,' " Marion recalls. "It was sort of a play on words, because once you get to know

Above: Just about everything in the Bates home has a story. The Advent wreath centerpiece was begun the first Christmas after Marion and David were married, almost 35 years ago. "Every Thanksgiving I would redo the wreath, leaving something from the year before," Marion says. She made the small herb tree on the bottom shelf of the hutch to coordinate with the wreath—a garland of silvery dried artemisia, globe amaranth, straw flowers, cockscomb, and statice wrapped around a silk tree. The impressive pewter collection began when she inherited a family teapot that dates back to 1840. Her great-great-great-grandmother was the original owner of the mulberry-colored English ironstone in the corner cupboard. The coverlet that adorns the dining table was a gift from Marion's sister, in appreciation for Marion's decorations at her daughter's wedding.

Opposite: "There's not a craft I haven't tried," Marion contends, "but my favorites are quilting, embroidery, and knitting." Examples of her crafts highlight every room. She made the hearth rug from a primitive rooster design she found while experimenting with rug hooking. The mantel wreath, nestled in amongst blue spruce and white pine, was made by attaching juniper, yarrow, goldenrod, bramble rose hips, and gray moss to a heart-shaped basket. The Santa in the center was carved by friend and artist Walter Bryant of Ashborough, North Carolina. Pepper, a large long-haired cat known as a Maine coon, looks like more than a lapful.

Left: Even the chandelier merits some merriment for the holidays. Greenery boughs and clusters of rosebuds and hearts add festive accents. The hearts are cut from craft-foam, sprayed with adhesive, and then rolled in crushed herbs and spices.

herbs, they will make friends for you."

Marion has designed herb gardens in North Carolina and Pennsylvania and has formed two units of the Herb Society of America, in addition to working on a book about herbs. For friends and family, she even finds time to make bridal bouquets and other wedding decorations with herbs. And as if all of this weren't enough, Marion also has a monthly television show for the Berks County area and writes a column for the *Kutztown Patriot.*

"I love all living things—all growing things," Marion says. That love has kept her growing since her first garden by the brook.

Marion's Spice Ornaments

At Christmas Marion decorates several trees with herbs and handmade ornaments. In the fall she gathers a variety of pods, such as rose of Sharon, cotton, evening primrose, poppy, star anise, and cloves. Then she hot-glues them together or attaches them to sweet gum balls or craft-foam balls. She makes orange "ringlet-cicles" by winding strips of orange peel around pencils.

Below, Marion shares her recipe for the aromatic ornaments adorning the rosemary tree pictured on the opposite page:

Mix together one cup well-drained applesauce, one teaspoon each of ground orrisroot, allspice, cloves, and ginger, ½ teaspoon ground nutmeg, and one tablespoon of cinnamon. Pour ½ cup cinnamon into a pie tin. Roll one teaspoon of applesauce mixture in the cinnamon. As the applesauce dries, roll it into a ball. Place balls in a glass pie plate. Dry in oven for one hour at 150°. Using a large needle, poke a hole through each ball, but wait at least 24 hours to string. Thread needle with yarn and pull yarn through hole in spice ball; then run needle back through same hole, leaving a long loop of yarn on top. Tie loose ends in a large knot at the bottom. The loop on top is the hanger. If you like, add a yarn bow for decoration.

Above: For this double-ringed wreath, Marion started with dock and then added a second wreath of greenery and a bow. Silhouettes of cats prance inside.

15

Welcome to a Country Yuletide Feast

Currant-Glazed Cornish Hens
Nutty Wild Rice Combo
Sweet Potatoes and Oranges
in Honey-Butter Sauce
Brussels Sprouts-Swiss Cheese Timbales
Calico Salad Vinaigrette
Savory Pepper Bread Wreaths
Vanilla Crème Pastry Squares
(Menu serves 6.)

Gather round the table for a sumptuous holiday feast—country style. This delicious menu is equally appropriate for a Christmas Eve family supper, Christmas dinner with guests, or for any occasion during the holidays when you want to serve something special.

Our country-heart chair backs and place mats, filet-crocheted in a homey ecru cotton thread, are just the things to dress up your dining room. These lacy treasures are delightfully easy to make. You don't have to be a veteran crocheter to follow the charted pattern and simple instructions.

Currant-Glazed Cornish Hens

1 (12-ounce) jar red currant jelly
3 tablespoons orange juice
6 (1- to 1¼-pound) Cornish hens
1 teaspoon coarsely ground pepper
Dried apricot roses (optional)
Italian flat leaf parsley sprigs (optional)

Combine jelly and orange juice in a small nonaluminum saucepan; cook over low heat, stirring constantly, until jelly melts. Remove from heat and set aside.

Remove giblets from Cornish hens (reserve for use in other recipes). Rinse hens with cold water and pat dry. Close cavities and secure with wooden toothpicks; truss. Sprinkle hens

with pepper and place in a lightly greased roasting pan, breast side up. Bake hens at 350° for 1¼ hours or until juices run clear.

Baste the hens frequently with two-thirds of the jelly mixture during the last 30 minutes of baking time.

Arrange hens on a large serving platter and brush with remaining one-third jelly mixture. If desired, garnish platter with apricot roses and parsley. Yield: 6 servings.

Note: To make apricot roses for garnish, use a rolling pin to flatten 4 or 5 dried apricots for each rose. Wrap apricots around each other, shaping to resemble a rose; pinch stem ends to adhere.

Nutty Wild Rice Combo

¼ cup plus 2 tablespoons butter or
    margarine, divided
1 cup chopped walnuts
⅔ cup chopped green onions
2 (6-ounce) packages long grain and wild
    rice mix
4⅔ cups apple juice

Melt ¼ cup butter in a large saucepan over low heat; add chopped walnuts and sauté until golden. Drain sautéed walnuts on paper towels and set aside.

Add remaining 2 tablespoons butter to saucepan and melt over low heat; add onions and sauté until tender.

Stir in rice mix and prepare according to package directions, substituting apple juice for water and omitting butter. Stir walnuts into rice. Spoon onto serving platter and serve immediately. Yield: 6 servings.

Opposite: What would Christmas be without a table spread with mouth-watering dishes that are a feast for the eye as well as the palate? Serve these for a meal that's sure to be a hit: counterclockwise, from left, Calico Salad Vinaigrette, Sweet Potatoes and Oranges in Honey-Butter Sauce, Brussels Sprouts-Swiss Cheese Timbales, Currant-Glazed Cornish Hens on a bed of Nutty Wild Rice Combo, and Savory Pepper Bread Wreaths. The crocheted chair backs and place mats add a warm country touch to your table setting. Instructions are on page 20.

Sweet Potatoes and Oranges in Honey-Butter Sauce

3 medium-size sweet potatoes (about 2 pounds)
3 medium-size oranges (about 1¾ pounds)
¼ cup brandy
3 tablespoons honey
2 tablespoons orange juice
1 tablespoon plus 1½ teaspoons brown sugar
1½ teaspoons butter

Place sweet potatoes in a large Dutch oven; add water to cover. Cover and bring to a boil. Cook 15 to 20 minutes or until tender. Drain and let cool.

Peel oranges and cut into ¼-inch-thick slices, removing any seeds. Set orange slices aside.

Combine brandy, honey, orange juice, brown sugar, and butter in a small, heavy saucepan, stirring well. Cook over medium heat 8 to 10 minutes or until sugar dissolves and mixture thickens, stirring occasionally. Remove from heat and keep warm.

Peel cooled sweet potatoes and slice crosswise into ¼-inch-thick slices. Attractively arrange sliced sweet potatoes and oranges on a serving platter and brush with honey-butter sauce. Serve immediately. Yield: 6 servings.

Brussels Sprouts- Swiss Cheese Timbales

1 pound fresh brussels sprouts
1 cup water
1 cup diluted chicken broth, divided
3 tablespoons butter or margarine
2 tablespoons minced onion
¼ cup all-purpose flour
1 tablespoon sugar
2 tablespoons Dijon mustard
¼ teaspoon salt
¼ teaspoon white pepper
3 eggs
¾ cup (3 ounces) shredded Swiss cheese
Bibb lettuce leaves (optional)
1 (2-ounce) jar diced pimiento, drained

Wash brussels sprouts thoroughly in cold water and remove discolored leaves. Cut off stem ends and slash bottom of each sprout with a shallow X. Combine brussels sprouts and water in a medium saucepan; cover and bring to a boil. Boil 8 to 10 minutes or until brussels sprouts are tender; drain.

Set aside 4 brussels sprouts for garnish. Place remaining brussels sprouts and ¼ cup chicken broth in container of an electric blender or food processor; top with cover and process until smooth. Set aside.

Melt butter in a large saucepan over low heat; add onion and sauté until tender. Stir in flour and cook 1 minute, stirring constantly. Gradually add remaining ¾ cup chicken broth; cook over medium heat, stirring constantly, until thickened. Remove from heat and stir in sugar, mustard, salt, and white pepper.

Beat eggs at medium speed of an electric mixer until thick and lemon colored. Gradually stir about one-fourth of the hot mixture into eggs; add to remaining hot mixture in saucepan, stirring constantly. Add pureed brussels sprout mixture and cheese. Cook over low heat, stirring constantly, until cheese melts. Remove from heat.

Divide mixture evenly among 6 lightly greased 6-ounce custard cups. Place cups in a 13- x 9- x 2-inch baking dish; pour hot water to a depth of 1 inch into dish. Bake at 350° for 55 to 60 minutes or until a knife inserted in center comes out clean. Remove cups from water and cool 5 minutes; invert onto a lettuce-lined serving platter, if desired. Remove smallest leaves from reserved brussels sprouts and arrange on timbales to form a flower design, using diced pimiento as center. Serve immediately. Yield: 6 servings.

Calico Salad Vinaigrette

2 (6-ounce) jars marinated artichoke hearts, undrained
¼ cup vegetable oil
¼ cup white wine vinegar
1 clove garlic, minced
¼ teaspoon dried whole basil
⅛ teaspoon lemon-pepper seasoning
24 Bibb lettuce leaves (about 2 small heads)
12 red leaf lettuce leaves (about 1 small head)
6 large radishes, cut into julienne strips

Drain artichoke hearts, reserving ¼ cup of the marinade. Coarsely chop the artichokes and set aside.

Combine reserved marinade, oil, white wine vinegar, minced garlic, dried whole basil, and lemon-pepper seasoning in a jar. Cover tightly and shake jar vigorously. Refrigerate vinaigrette mixture until thoroughly chilled.

Arrange 4 Bibb lettuce leaves and 2 red leaf lettuce leaves on each of 6 salad plates. Top each of the lettuce servings with chopped artichokes and sprinkle with radish strips. Shake vinaigrette mixture well and pour evenly over salads. Yield: 6 servings.

Savory Pepper Bread Wreaths

1 package dry yeast
½ teaspoon sugar
½ cup warm beer (105° to 115°)
1½ cups all-purpose flour, divided
2 tablespoons vegetable oil
½ teaspoon salt
½ teaspoon coarsely ground pepper
1 egg, beaten

Dissolve the yeast and sugar in the warm beer in a large bowl; let mixture stand 5 minutes. Add ¾ cup flour, oil, salt, and pepper. Beat at medium speed of an electric mixer 2 minutes. Stir in remaining ¾ cup flour to make a soft dough.

Turn dough out onto a lightly floured surface and knead until smooth and elastic (about 8 to 10 minutes). Shape into a ball and place in a well-greased bowl, turning to grease top. Cover and let rise in a warm place (85°), free from drafts, 1 hour or until doubled in bulk.

Punch dough down and divide into 12 equal portions, shaping each into a 14-inch rope. Fold each rope in half and pinch ends to seal. Twist each rope and pinch ends together to form a wreath.

Place wreaths 1½ inches apart on a lightly greased baking sheet. Cover wreaths and let rise in a warm place (85°), free from drafts, for 30 minutes or until doubled in bulk. Gently brush each wreath with egg and bake at 400° for 15 to 20 minutes or until golden brown. Yield: 1 dozen.

Vanilla Crème Pastry Squares

½ (17¼-ounce) package frozen puff pastry, thawed
2 cups cranberry juice cocktail
⅔ cup sugar
3 tablespoons cornstarch
2 tablespoons Chambord
  or other raspberry-flavored
  liqueur
4 egg yolks
½ cup sugar
2 tablespoons all-purpose flour
1¼ cups milk
2 teaspoons butter or margarine
2 teaspoons vanilla extract
Powdered sugar
Fresh cranberries (optional)
Fresh mint sprigs (optional)

Roll the thawed puff pastry into a 13- x 9-inch rectangle on a lightly floured surface; cut pastry into six 4-inch squares. Transfer the squares to a lightly greased baking sheet and bake at 450° for 3 to 4 minutes or until pastry is puffed and golden brown. Remove from oven and set aside.

Combine cranberry juice cocktail, ⅔ cup sugar, cornstarch, and liqueur in a small, heavy saucepan, stirring with a wire whisk until well blended.

Bring to a boil and boil 1 minute or until mixture thickens, stirring constantly. Remove from heat and let cool.

Combine egg yolks and ½ cup sugar in a medium saucepan. Add flour, stirring with wire whisk to blend. Gradually stir in milk. Cook over medium heat, stirring constantly with wire whisk, just until mixture comes to a boil. Reduce heat and cook 1 minute. Remove from heat; add butter and vanilla, stirring until butter melts.

To assemble each dessert, spoon cranberry juice mixture evenly onto 6 dessert plates. Split pastry squares in half horizontally. Spoon vanilla crème mixture evenly into cavities of 6 halves; cover with remaining halves.

Sift powdered sugar over the top of each of the crème-filled pastry squares and carefully transfer them to dessert plates. If desired, garnish the pastry squares with fresh cranberries and mint. Yield: 6 servings.

Right: A Vanilla Crème Pastry Square nestled in a fabulous berry-flavored sauce wraps up this country feast. But don't put away your crocheted country-heart accessories. Leave them out for family and visitors to enjoy all year long.

Country-Heart Filet Crochet

Materials for one chair back:
chart on page 135
1 ball #10 ecru cotton crochet thread
size 3 steel crochet hook

CHAIR BACK: *Row 1:* Ch 6, join with 1 dc in beg ch. Turn work. *Row 2:* Ch 6, 1 dc in dc of previous row, (3 dc, ch 2, tr) in ch-6 sp; turn work. *Row 3:* Ch 6, 1 dc in tr, 2 dc in ch-2 sp, ch 2, 1 tr in ch-6 sp; turn work. *Rows 4-33:* Continue following chart as established. To inc 1 st at beg of row, ch 6, 1 dc in tr of previous row. To inc 1 st at end of row, ch 2, 1 tr in ch-6 sp. To inc 2 sts at beg of row, ch 2 extra sts. To inc 2 sts at end of row, work the extra sts as tr and fasten into side of previous st. On rows with no beg inc, ch 5 (counts as 1 dc, ch 2). To dec at beg of row, sl st over to 2nd square of row, ch 5 (counts as 2 dc, ch 2). To dec at end of row, leave last square of row unworked. *Rows 34-37:* Lobes of heart are worked separately. To work top of right lobe of heart, sl st over to 2nd square of row 34, ch 5, and follow chart across to center of heart; turn work. After row 37 of chart, fasten off. Join thread at center of heart to complete top of left lobe in the same manner. Do not fasten off after row 37 of chart.

EDGING: *Row 1:* Sc around heart. *Row 2:* * Ch 4, (1 sc in next st, ch 1) 3 times, rep from * around. *Row 3:* * (1 dc, ch 1) 7 times in ch-4 sp, ch 1, 1 sc in center sc, ch 1, rep from * around. Fasten off.

TIES (make 4): Join thread just below edging at points indicated on chart. Ch 125; turn work. Work 1 sc in each ch. Fasten off.

Materials for one place mat:
chart on page 135
2 balls #10 ecru cotton crochet thread
size 3 steel or D aluminum crochet hook
2 balls #20 cotton crochet thread

PLACE MAT: Follow directions for chair back, except work with 2 strands of #10 cotton crochet thread held tog as one. Work edging as for chair back with 2 strands of #20 cotton crochet thread held tog as one.

Standard Crochet Abbreviations

beg—beginning
ch—chain
dc—double crochet
dec—decrease
inc—increase

rep—repeat
sc—single crochet
sl—slip
sp—space
st(s)—stitch(es)

tog—together
tr—triple crochet
*—repeat instructions following
    asterisk as indicated

All Through the House

Holiday motifs suitable for a variety of uses can be hard to find. Here are just such unpretentious, yet ingenious, shapes: a fir tree, an inviting cottage, and some playful reindeer. These clean, basic forms are ideal to group on pillows, wooden blocks, Christmas gift wrap, or even a festive wall hanging.

Wooden House Blocks

Materials:
patterns on page 134
scraps of pine 2 x 4
saw
medium-grade sandpaper
flat latex paints: brick red, forest green,
  beige, and black, or colors of choice
1″ paintbrushes

Transfer Wooden House Block patterns to wood and cut out. Sand all edges; then paint to match blocks in photograph on opposite page, or as desired. Allow to dry.

Appliquéd Pillows

Materials to make three pillows:
patterns and placement diagrams on
  page 134
tissue paper
¼ yard (45″-wide) each of red, green,
  muslin, and black cotton fabrics for
  appliqués
½ yard (45″-wide) muslin for background
thread to match
1 yard (45″-wide) green checkerboard fabric
½ yard (45″-wide) red checkerboard fabric
3 (16″-square) pillow forms

Transfer patterns to tissue paper. Pin tissue paper patterns to fabric and cut out, adding ¼″ seam allowances. From muslin, cut three 13″ squares. Referring to placement diagrams on page 134, pin appliqués to muslin squares. Turning under seam allowances, appliqué pieces. Add stars, doors, and windows last.

From red checkerboard, cut 2 strips, 3″ x 13″, for side borders, and 2 strips, 3″ x 17″, for top and bottom borders. From green checkerboard, cut 4 strips, 3″ x 13″, for side borders, and 4 strips, 3″ x 17″, for top and bottom borders.

With right sides facing, sew one red checkerboard side border to each side of a muslin square, using ½″ seams. Then, with right sides facing, sew red checkerboard top and bottom borders to top and bottom of square, matching corners and using ½″ seams. Repeat with green checkerboard borders for remaining 2 pillows.

Cut 2 red and 4 green checkerboard back pieces, 10″ x 17″. Sew a ½″ hem along one long edge of each back piece. (See Diagram 1 on this page.) With right sides facing, pin the 2 red checkerboard back pieces to the pillow front with the red checkerboard border, overlapping hemmed edges at center back to form a 17″ x 17″ square. (See Diagram 2 on this page.) Stitch all around square, using ½″ seam. (An opening will remain at center where back pieces overlap.) Trim corners and turn. Insert pillow form. Repeat with green checkerboard backs for 2 remaining pillows.

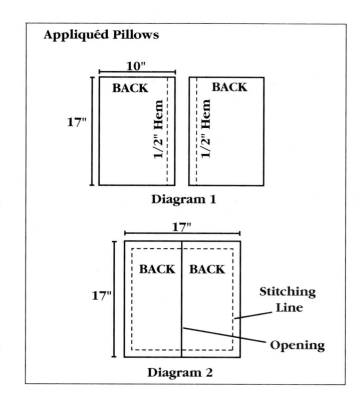

Appliquéd Pillows

Diagram 1

Diagram 2

Above: These country-stenciled packages offer another use for the house and tree patterns on page 134. Choose acrylic paints in your favorite holiday colors; then stencil designs with a stencil brush. Wrap your packages first so that you can place the design right where it's needed. For a finishing touch, tear strips of coordinating cotton fabric to make casual country ribbons.

Above: This wall hanging sports a herd of calico reindeer. It's quite versatile—try it as a table runner, too.

Reindeer Wall Quilt

Materials:
patterns on pages 134–135
⅜ yard paper-backed fusible web
scraps of brown cotton prints and solids for deer
scraps of green cotton prints for trees
scrap of muslin for star
⅛ yard (45″-wide) solid black cotton fabric for antlers and tree trunks
½ yard (45″-wide) osnaburg or other rough cotton fabric for background
⅓ yard (45″-wide) dark green plaid for border
½ yard (45″-wide) brown cotton print for backing
½ yard low-loft batting
22 (½″) ecru buttons
ecru embroidery floss

Note: All seams are ¼″.

Trace patterns onto paper side of fusible web and cut out as directed. Following manufacturer's instructions, iron web to wrong side of desired fabrics and cut out.

Cut background fabric 37″ x 13½″. Referring to photograph for placement, position appliqués right side up and fuse to background, according to manufacturer's instructions, in the following order: For deer, fuse antlers to fabric and then body; fuse trunk and then tree to background. Add star to top of one tree as in photograph.

From border fabric, cut 2 strips, 3¾″ x 37″, for top and bottom borders, and 2 strips, 3¾″ x 20″, for sides. With right sides facing, stitch top and bottom borders to background. Then stitch side borders. Press seams toward border.

Cut batting and backing 42½″ x 19″. Stack, in this order: quilt top (right side down), batting, and backing (right side up). Pin. Position buttons as desired and sew to quilt front through all layers with 6 strands of floss, tying knot on back. Cut floss 1″ from knot. One or 2 knots can be tied on front of quilt, if desired.

Turn ½″ of border edges to back and press. Turn under ¼″ and slipstitch to backing. Finished width of borders is 3″.

Finished quilt measures 42½″ x 19″.

24

Santa Fe Wreaths

Across the city of Santa Fe, influences of Spanish and Indian cultures abound. During the Christmas season, these influences are seen in the variety of wreaths adorning doorways throughout the city. Thick strands of chilies, known as *ristras,* from the fall harvest hang to one side of gates that lead to hidden courtyards. In this state with its wealth of natural materials, wreaths made of dried native plants flourish.

A little Indian village north of Santa Fe, known as Velarde, is home to Loretta and Herman Valdez. Loretta and her staff have arranged chilies, gourds, corn, and other natural materials into *ristras* and wreaths for more than 25 years. Other designers, florists, and Christmas enthusiasts also gather peppergrass and corn husks during the fall, in preparation for the holiday wreath making to come.

Throughout Santa Fe, delicate wrought iron gates, rough-hewn doors with carved figures, and bright spots of southwestern color all speak of an inner individuality behind the uniform adobe exteriors. At Christmas, festive wreaths suggest the interior enchantment of the season.

Above: Little peppers called chili piquin dance around this heart-shaped wreath, inviting visitors through a gate to a courtyard in the old district of Santa Fe. The gnarled branches above the gate are part of what is reputed to be the oldest wisteria vine in the city. The wreath was made by Sandy Worth of Embudo, New Mexico.

Left: Red chilies gathered during the fall harvest decorate many doors and gates in Santa Fe throughout the holidays. Long fat strings of chilies, known as ristras, *hang from adobe walls. Here, bits of frayed corn husk add to the southwestern flavor of this chili wreath.*

25

Right: This wreath is another made by Sandy Worth. The small dried green flowers circling the pine needle wreath are named for their aroma—chocolate. "When you're out in the garden and all of a sudden you get a whiff of a hot fudge sundae, you know some chocolate flowers are nearby," Sandy says. A floral designer and farmer, Sandy grows or gathers all the materials for her wreaths in New Mexico.

Below: Coyote fences surround many Santa Fe adobes. Built from thin branches and slim tree trunks, the fences were originally made to keep out coyotes. The giant wreath is an expansion of the traditional chili wreath. Sandy Worth created the wreath by arranging German statice, rice grass, white fluffy peppergrass, and chilies.

Left: Created by Rex Mason of Santa Fe, this airy wreath is quite a surprise. Rex fashioned it by thinly wrapping papier-mâché over pieces of fruit. Before the papier-mâché dried completely, he slipped the fruit out through delicate incisions. Then he wired the white, light fruit shapes, along with leaf-shaped pieces of tin, to a papier-mâché wreath form. The exquisite curves of the wrought iron inset of this gate are representative of the variety apparent in the entranceways of Santa Fe.

27

Celebrate the Season With Miniwreaths

These miniature versions of the traditional wreath will add a yuletide welcome to every nook and cranny of your home.

Above: Brown, spiky sweet gum balls, hot-glued into a variety of shapes and sizes, become country-charming miniwreaths.

Below: Corn husk miniwreaths, embellished with colored strips of raffia and dried red peppers, add a southwestern flair to the season.

Left: Raid your button box and ribbon bag for little bits of whimsy. Glue them onto purchased or handmade miniwreaths to give sparkle to forgotten corners of your home.

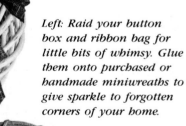

Above: Glue tiny ribbon roses to purchased two-inch vine wreaths for quick and adorable ornaments, package toppers, or napkin rings.

Below: Sumac berries, tied with a red plaid ribbon, turn a twig wreath into a treasure. Underneath it, a staunch nutcracker soldier stands guard over a mini, made by hot-gluing mixed nuts onto a wreath form.

Ornaments from Nature

Nature is an abundant source of materials for holiday decorating. Summer fields offer many beautiful grasses. Gather them in midsummer, before they go to seed. Harvest small grains, such as millet, wheat, oats, and barley, before their seeds drop.

Pick seed pods of tulips, daylilies, and peonies in summer, when they're green, or in early fall, when they're mature. Wild plants, such as milkweed, sweet gum, and sumac, yield pods that add a country touch to wreaths, garlands, and table arrangements.

Don't forget pinecones. They usually drop in midsummer and should be collected before their color fades. Nuts like acorns, chestnuts, beechnuts, and hickory nuts can also add warmth to holiday decorations.

A Country Christmas Pantry

SERVE UP SOME SWEET DELIGHTS

♥

SUGAR 'N SPICE
AND GINGERBREAD'S NICE

♥

COUNTRY MARKET GIFT IDEAS

♥

TABLETOPS FROM THE PANTRY

♥

A CALICO BEAR WITH CANDY TREATS

♥

IDEAS: FESTIVE TRIMS
FOR TASTY FARE

Serve Up Some Sweet Delights

Country entertaining during the Christmas holidays means a sideboard filled with sweet delights. And it's true—the more cakes and icings there are, the merrier the season.

Here's some merriment for the holidays that couldn't be sweeter. First, there's a luscious chocolate treat that's smothered with cherries and dressed in whipped cream. (Etch the elegant cake cover in the photograph by following the simple instructions.)

Next comes a batch of festive fruitcakes just the right size for gifts—or your own enjoyment. There's nothing ordinary about these fruitcakes; cinnamon, nutmeg, allspice, and liqueur blend with applesauce to make an unusually moist and flavorful delicacy. With a dozen miniature cakes per recipe, you can try all the suggested garnishes and even create a few new ones of your very own.

Chocolate-Cherry Cola Cake

1 (18.25-ounce) package devil's food cake mix with pudding
1 (10-ounce) bottle cherry cola-flavored carbonated beverage
1 (21-ounce) can cherry pie filling, chilled
1 (16-ounce) carton frozen whipped topping, thawed

Prepare and bake cake mix according to package directions, substituting cherry cola for water and using two 9-inch round cake pans. Place one cake layer on a cake platter; spread with half of cherry pie filling and top with second cake layer. Spread a small amount of whipped topping around sides of cake to seal filling and crumbs. Set remaining pie filling and whipped topping aside.

Spoon half of whipped topping into a pastry bag fitted with a No. 2B basket-weave tip. Pipe vertical lines of whipped topping around sides of cake. Fit pastry bag with a No. 6B star tip and spoon remaining whipped topping into bag. Pipe a shell design around base and top outer edge of cake. Spoon remaining pie filling onto top of cake, gently spreading to edge of shell border. Cover and refrigerate until thoroughly chilled. Yield: one 2-layer cake.

Etched Cake Cover

Materials:
stencil pattern on page 136
clear glass cake stand with cover
peel-and-stick vinyl shelf covering
grease pencil
craft knife
wide masking tape
wax paper
etching cream
soft-bristled paintbrush

Wash cake cover and dry thoroughly. Transfer rose stencil to a piece of peel-and-stick vinyl shelf covering. Do not remove waxed backing from vinyl yet.

Holding uncut stencil against the cake cover, mark correct placement with a grease pencil. Place the stencil on a smooth, flat piece of cardboard and use a craft knife to carefully cut away all the stencil sections that show as white on pattern.

Lay stencil face down. Slowly and carefully peel off the entire waxed backing. If any stencil pieces stick to the backing sheet, stop and press the backing sheet back down onto the stencil until the loose piece is lying flat again.

Hold the stencil at each end so that the exposed adhesive side is facing down. Bend up the 2 sides of the stencil so that the center is bowed down. Using your previously marked guide for placement, carefully apply stencil to the cake cover. (The bowed center of the stencil should touch the cover first.) Then, beginning in the center of the design, use the palm of your hand to smooth out the stencil to the left and then to the right.

Place a piece of wax paper over the stencil on the cake cover. With the palm of your hand, press firmly in a back-and-forth and then up-and-down motion. (This will ensure that all the stencil pieces are lying flat and are perfectly adhered to the glass.)

Opposite: The grand pairing of a Chocolate-Cherry Cola Cake and a cake cover etched with roses can make quite an impressive holiday gift. The lucky recipient need never know you made them both so quickly.

Tape strips of masking tape to exposed surfaces around the outside of the stencil to protect the surfaces from the etching process.

Make sure that the areas to be etched are free from grease, dirt, fingerprints, or any adhesive residue and that the glass, room, and the etching cream are at least 65° F.

To etch design, use the brush to apply a thick coat of etching cream over the cutout design of the stencil. Make sure all exposed areas inside the stencil are covered with etching cream. Leave cream on 5–10 minutes. Use brush to redistribute cream as necessary to keep all exposed glass covered. After 5–10 minutes, wash cream off with tap water. Remove stencil.

Note: For information on how to order a precut rose stencil, see source listing on page 154.

Above: Dress these little fruitcakes with a simple touch or an elegant flourish. Either way, they'll make a great impression.

Applesauce Mini-Fruitcakes

1½ cups applesauce
1 cup sugar
½ cup butter or margarine
1 (8-ounce) package red candied cherries, chopped
1 (8-ounce) package green candied cherries, chopped
1 (8-ounce) package pitted dates, chopped
¾ cup raisins
2 cups chopped pecans
2¼ cups all-purpose flour
2 teaspoons baking soda
½ teaspoon salt
1¼ teaspoons ground cinnamon
½ teaspoon ground nutmeg
¼ teaspoon ground allspice
1½ teaspoons vanilla extract
¾ cup fruit-flavored liqueur
Assorted garnishes (optional)
Glaze (recipe follows)

Combine first 3 ingredients in a heavy saucepan; simmer 5 minutes, stirring constantly to dissolve sugar. Remove from heat and let cool.

Combine fruit and pecans in a large bowl. Combine dry ingredients; add to fruit mixture, stirring well. Stir in applesauce mixture and vanilla. Spoon into well-greased Bundt muffin pans, filling two-thirds full. Bake at 350° for 25 to 30 minutes or until a wooden pick inserted in center comes out clean. Cool in pans 5 minutes. Remove and cool completely on wire racks. Sprinkle cakes evenly with liqueur.

If desired, garnish cakes with cranberries coated in melted red currant jelly or with crystallized violets garnished with mint. Or drizzle cakes with glaze and top a few with toasted sliced almonds and candied cherries arranged to form a flower design. Decorate remaining glazed cakes with mandarin orange slices; garnish with mint. Yield: 1 dozen mini-fruitcakes.

Glaze:

3 cups sifted powdered sugar
¼ cup plus 2 tablespoons milk

Combine sugar and milk, beating until smooth. Use immediately. Yield: about 1½ cups.

Sugar 'n Spice and Gingerbread's Nice

New candies and cookies on the market shelves always catch Debbie's eye. She envisions how they'll look as sugar-coated roof shingles or stepping stones leading to a candy cottage.

Above: Students from Nelson-Dewey Elementary School in Superior, Wisconsin, are drawn by the fantasy of the sugared houses. Debbie spent more than 80 hours over a six-week period to complete the replica of the Fairlawn Museum. The gingerbread ornaments on the tree behind Debbie were made from a cookie cutter she designed in the shape of the museum.

For seven holiday seasons in a row, Debbie Welter shopped for gumdrops, tiny candy hearts, and ice-cream cones. She used the sundries every year to decorate a different Christmas house she had made—a cottage of gingerbread, for instance, or a log cabin of pretzels, or even a fairy castle raised from simple sugar cubes.

Things could have continued this way Christmas after Christmas except for one thing—Debbie has a true architect's philosophy. "I like to give myself challenges," she says.

A challenge was just what she got a couple of years ago when the Douglas County Historical Society decided to decorate a local landmark, the Fairlawn House and Museum, in Debbie's hometown of Superior, Wisconsin. Impressed with her efforts in various crafts, the historical society asked for her help. She not only agreed to decorate the 1890 Victorian museum with several of her confection cottages, but she also took the idea a step further. She built a miniature replica of the museum itself—this one held together with frosting instead of mortar!

Debbie originally wanted to build the structure of gingerbread, but she knew from experience that chilled dough tends to shrink and buckle during baking. This tendency can be accommodated in a quaint cottage, but a large model with 80 windows needs flawless surfaces. Debbie also felt a museum wall needed more support than a cookie could give.

After hours of experimentation, she found the perfect museum wall—corrugated cardboard frosted with an imitation gingerbread concoction of crushed graham crackers, water, egg whites, and spices. She created amber-colored windows, pouring them from a candy mixture of sugar and corn syrup, and decorated each one with its

own tiny frosting wreath.

The museum replica's tall tower took its shape from a thoughtful contribution. The museum's director gave Debbie the mailing tube that once held the original plans of the museum. So the turret not only has an accurate circular shape, but it literally stands on its own history.

Debbie's three children, Brian, Betsy, and Steven, are, like most citizens of Superior, big fans of her work—but for a different reason. "They eat the houses I make so I can make a new one the next year," Debbie says with a laugh. "That's the biggest help they can give me."

Country Market Gift Ideas

Homemade gifts are the best kind. They say, "You're special," to the person who receives them. And nothing is more welcome at Christmastime than delights from the kitchen.

On the following pages, you'll find a bumper crop of gourmet gift ideas that will assure you a reputation as a thoughtful giver. Recipes are as easy to prepare as they are tasty and can be made well in advance of the last-minute Christmas rush.

You'll discover that part of the fun of making and giving snacks and condiments from your kitchen is finding just the right container in which to present the gift. Recycle instant coffee jars and store-bought jam containers. Comb yard sales and flea markets for interesting and inexpensive jars, bottles, baskets, and tins.

After they've been filled with your culinary crafts, add a country touch to each container with a simple calico jar topper, a festive citrus garland, or a spicy ginger miniwreath. You'll have a bounty of gifts that is sure to bring compliments from your lucky friends who receive them.

Hurry-Up Brandied Fruit

1 (17-ounce) can apricot halves, drained
1 (16-ounce) can pear halves, drained
1 (16-ounce) can sliced peaches, drained
1 (16-ounce) can seedless grapes, drained
1 (15¼-ounce) can unsweetened pineapple chunks, drained
1 (11-ounce) can mandarin oranges, drained
1 (6-ounce) jar maraschino cherries, drained
1½ cups brandy
1½ cups honey

Combine first 7 ingredients in a large bowl; toss gently to mix. Combine brandy and honey, stirring with a wire whisk until well blended; pour over fruit and stir gently to coat well. Cover and let stand at room temperature 8 hours to blend flavors. Stir mixture occasionally.

Serve brandied fruit over ice cream or pound cake. Yield: 9½ cups.

Note: Hurry-Up Brandied Fruit can be packaged for gift giving in decorative jars with airtight lids and stored at room temperature up to 2 weeks.

Holiday Traveler Snack Mix

1 (3½-ounce) can flaked coconut
1 (16-ounce) can salted peanuts
1 (16-ounce) package candy-coated chocolate pieces
1 (16-ounce) package 100% natural cereal with raisins and dates

Spread coconut evenly on a baking sheet. Bake at 350° for 10 minutes or until lightly toasted, stirring after 5 minutes. Remove from oven and let cool.

Combine toasted coconut, peanuts, chocolate pieces, and cereal, tossing gently. Store snack mix in an airtight container. Yield: 10½ cups.

Garlic-Flavored Olive Oil

12 large cloves garlic, peeled
2 (6-inch) wooden skewers
4 cups olive oil
4 fresh oregano sprigs

Thread 6 cloves of garlic onto each skewer. Insert a skewer of garlic into each of 2 sterilized pint bottles, measuring at least 7 inches in height. Set aside.

Warm oil over medium heat until hot, not boiling; pour immediately into bottles, using a funnel, if necessary. Allow oil to cool to room temperature. Insert 2 sprigs of oregano into each bottle; cover tightly and store in refrigerator at least 24 hours to blend flavors. Allow oil to reach room temperature before using to sauté vegetables or chicken. Yield: 4 cups.

Gift-Givers' Roasted Peppers

12 medium-size sweet red peppers (about 4½ pounds)
¼ cup plus 2 tablespoons lemon juice
1 tablespoon salt

Wash and dry peppers. Cut into thirds lengthwise; remove and discard stems, seeds, and membranes. Place peppers, skin sides up, on baking sheets; flatten peppers with palm of hand. Broil peppers 3 inches from heat 2 to 3 minutes or until skins are blackened and charred. Immediately transfer peppers to a large brown paper bag and roll top tightly to trap steam. Allow peppers to steam 5 minutes. Slowly unroll top to let steam escape; carefully remove peppers. Remove and discard skins.

Cut peppers into ¾-inch squares; pack into hot, sterilized half-pint jars, leaving ½ inch headspace. Add 1 tablespoon lemon juice and ½ teaspoon salt to each jar. Cover peppers with boiling water, leaving ½ inch headspace; remove

Above: Citrus peel, gingerroot, and cinnamon sticks make aromatic trims for your homemade kitchen gifts: Gift-Givers' Roasted Peppers (small jars), Raspberry-Wine Vinegar (corked bottle), Garlic-Flavored Olive Oil (bottle with stopper), Hurry-Up Brandied Fruit (large jars), Holiday Traveler Snack Mix (wooden bucket), Herbal Honey Sauce (medium jar with calico bonnet). See the following page for garland and wreath instructions.

air bubbles and wipe jar rims. Cover at once with metal lids and screw on bands. Process in a pressure canner at 10 pounds pressure (240°) for 35 minutes. Roasted peppers can be used in pimiento cheese, spaghetti sauce, Spanish rice, or as a topping for pizza or casseroles. Yield: 6 half pints.

Raspberry-Wine Vinegar

1 (10-ounce) package frozen raspberries in
  light syrup, thawed and undrained
2 cups red wine vinegar (5% acidity)
⅔ cup Burgundy or other dry red wine

Place raspberries in a strainer positioned over
a small bowl; let stand 10 minutes to collect
juice. Remove raspberries from strainer and reserve for use in other recipes. Line strainer with
several layers of cheesecloth; strain juice to
yield ½ cup clear juice.

Combine ½ cup raspberry juice, vinegar, and
Burgundy, stirring to blend. Pour vinegar mixture into decorative bottles or jars, using a funnel, if necessary; cork each bottle tightly. Let
mixture stand at room temperature at least 8
hours to blend flavors before serving over salad
greens. Yield: 3⅓ cups.

Note: Raspberry-Wine Vinegar can be stored in
a cool, dark place up to 6 months.

Herbal Honey Sauce

1 cup honey
¼ cup finely chopped fresh lemon balm
2 tablespoons lemon juice

Combine all ingredients, stirring well. Pour
honey sauce into an airtight container. Let stand
at room temperature at least 8 hours to blend
flavors before serving on biscuits, broiled beef,
pork, or chicken. Stir well before serving. Yield:
about 1¼ cups.

To top it off . . .

Use your imagination
and materials you
have on hand to add
a bit of country
whimsy to your spe-
cial homemade gifts.
Used with simple fab-
ric bonnets or all on
their own, these col-
orful and fragrant jar
and bottle toppers
complement your
best recipes.

Citrus Garlands

Quarter several large unblemished oranges,
cutting from top to bottom with a sharp par-
ing knife. Pull peel from fruit in large sections. (Reserve fruit for other purposes.) Cut
out shapes from peel, using 2″ or smaller
cookie cutters or a craft knife. Using a small
leather punch, make holes in peel for decorative effect, or to aid in stringing garlands.
Lay shapes on cookie sheet and place away
from direct sunlight. Let dry for several days.
Turn shapes over when they begin to curl.

For garland, thread desired length of ¹⁄₁₆″-
wide satin ribbon or pearl cotton through a
long needle and assemble shapes, alternating
rind with wooden beads or cinnamon sticks.

Gingerroot Wreath

Slice whole, fresh gingerroot into ⅛″-thick
slices, using sharp knife. For wreath, insert
desired length of thin florists' wire through
centers of slices, leaving space between
slices to aid in drying. Allow to dry 3 to 4
days. When dry, pack slices closely together
along wire. Bend wire to form wreath, twisting ends to join. Clip excess wire with wire
cutters. Add ribbon hanger. Decorate with
spices or a dried orange peel ornament.

Aromatic Simmer

Don't discard those citrus peels! Use them to
make a simmering medley of Christmas
scents instead. Combine peels with 2 cinnamon sticks, one teaspoon each whole cloves
and whole nutmeg, and one cup water in a
saucepan. Bring to a boil; then simmer
slowly, adding water as necessary.

Tabletops from The Pantry

Even the smallest corners of the house deserve to sparkle at Christmastime. With so many little spaces to embellish, the search is on for new ideas. But where to look?

The pantry is really a natural source for all kinds of wonderful, original ornament ideas. Wooden spoons, tiny tart tins, and tea infusers all take on a new decorative role. And tabletops offer the perfect pint-sized spot for these newly discovered ornaments.

The Baker's Tree, the Tea Tree, and the Wooden Spoon Tree all show off the charms of the pantry. Take our lead; then try other ideas on your own. Possibilities line the shelves.

The Baker's Tree

Any shining kitchen item becomes a star on these little boughs of cedar. Hot-glue ribbons to the sides of tin custard cups, candy molds, tart tins, and cookie press templates and see how they sparkle.

Sheaves of oats, dressed in red and green, adorn this tree. And small bottles of flavoring, such as vanilla, do their part. Kumquats and cranberries make a garland that draws the eye from one ornament to the next.

Above: Cookie cutters circle the base of this shaggy cedar, awaiting their turn to shine in the spotlight. The fruit garland is strung on fishing line for extra strength.

Wee Walnut Baskets

These baskets may be small enough to carry just three cranberries, but they'll be in big demand this Christmas. It's only a little trouble, too, to make a nice *big* basketful.

Most craft stores offer small motorized hobby tools with grinding surfaces or saw blades. These are extremely useful in any craft requiring precision cutting on fragile or brittle materials, such as nutshells. You will need to use one of these tools to transform the walnut shells into basket shapes.

Follow the natural seam of the shell, making a vertical cut about 1/8″ to each side of the seam. Continue the cuts to the center of the nutshell to form the basket handle. Then cut horizontally across the midsection of the shell, stopping at the handle. After making the cuts, remove all nut meat with a pick. Grind down any rough spots inside the shell for a finished surface.

39

Above: Made from soft cotton tea towels, the heart-shaped ornaments add a bright touch to this tabletop tree. The matching teapot, cup, creamer, and sugar bowl are pieces from a 1920s tea set.

The Tea Tree

This Christmas, add an old-fashioned pastime— teatime—to your busy schedule. Unpack your childhood tea set—if your mother can part with it. Gather the tiny cups around for inspiration; then make a list of the items you'll want to add to your Tea Tree.

We've chosen tea infusers in clever shapes, like teapots and teaspoons. Tie lengths of ribbon to these, and you have instant tabletop ornaments. Tea tins, available in various sizes, and miniature jam jars also make quick ornaments. And when the time comes, you have the makings right at hand for the tea party you deserve.

40

Tea Towel Heart Ornaments

Materials;
pattern on page 135
plaid or checked cotton tea towels
contrasting thread
plastic or cardboard template material
polyester stuffing
16″ (⅛″-wide) ribbon for each ornament in
   colors to match sewing thread
long straight pin or quilting pin

Wash tea towels and iron if needed. Transfer the heart pattern to template material. Lay template on single layer of towel, placing on straight grain as indicated. Cut out heart. Cut another heart for back.

Place wrong sides of hearts together. Using a ⅛″ zigzag stitch and contrasting thread, sew through all layers of fabric on stitching line, leaving opening as indicated for stuffing. Clip at top of heart as indicated. Stuff lightly and zigzag-stitch opening closed.

Fringe all around heart by pulling threads down to zigzag stitching. Use the long straight pin or quilting pin to separate threads for pulling. To make fringe fluffier, pin ornament to a towel and wash. Trim the fringe to even off rounded edges.

Cut the ribbon in half. Make a loop with one half. Tack loop to back of heart ornament for hanger. Tie a small bow with the other half of ribbon. Tack bow to front of ornament as shown in photograph.

Wooden Spoon Tree

Materials:
9 (12″) wooden kitchen spoons
22″ (1″-diameter) wooden dowel
1¾″ wooden toy wheel
¾″ x 6″ wooden circle for base
electric drill with ½″ and ¾″ butterfly bits
saw
wood glue
fine-grade sandpaper
oil or clear varnish, if desired

Note: If you intend to apply a finish to the tree, lightly sand all pieces before gluing.

Above: This spoon tree will cause quite a stir when decorated with homemade or store-bought cookies and cookie cutters tied with bright holiday ribbon.

Cut spoons, measuring from the tip of the bowl, as follows: one at 5¼″, 2 each at 7¼″, 8¾″, 10¼″, and 11½″.

Drill a ¾″ hole, ½″ deep, in center of base.

Using a ruler and pencil, lightly draw a straight line down length of dowel as a guide. Perpendicular to this line, mark dowel 3½″ from top. Mark again 4″ down dowel from 3½″ mark and twice more at 4″ intervals. Drill holes the diameter of spoon handles straight through the dowel at these 4 marks, making sure that all holes are perpendicular to the dowel.

Glue the toy wheel horizontally on top of dowel. Allow to dry. Drill a ½″-deep hole the diameter of the shortest spoon handle through the wheel and into the end of the dowel.

Drip a small amount of glue into hole in base. Insert bottom of dowel and let dry. Drip a small amount of glue into each dowel hole and insert spoon handles to form branches of tree, with the longest spoons at the bottom. (Make sure the bowls of the spoons face front.) Glue the 5¼″ spoon vertically into hole in wheel and dowel. Allow to dry. (If the fit is too tight, use sandpaper to sand down the spoon handles for a better fit.)

Apply oil or clear varnish finish, if desired.

Quick and Easy— But Oh, So Good!

You don't have to spend hours in the kitchen puzzling over complicated recipes in order to give fancy food gifts this Christmas. The following simple recipes are made with a minimum of ingredients.

Surprise someone with a jar of Spicy Pickled Pineapple or Christmas Brunch Jam. Stir up several batches of Mocha Mix in an Instant for all the chocolate lovers on your list. Some favorite friend will love to receive a bagful of Country Market Bean Mix in one of the whimsical appliquéd gift bags on page 45. (The no-stitch technique makes the appliqué a snap!)

And for gift tags, make your own, with cross-stitched quilt-block patterns like those shown on the opposite page.

Toasted Pecans on the Light Side

4 cups pecan halves
2 cups water
1/3 cup salt

Spread pecans evenly in bottom of a 12- x 8- x 2-inch nonaluminum baking dish. Combine water and salt, stirring to dissolve; pour over pecans and stir gently. Let them stand at room temperature 30 minutes. Drain off salted water.

Transfer pecans to paper towels to drain; blot excess moisture from pecans, using additional paper towels. Let them stand at room temperature 2 hours to dry. Arrange pecans in a single layer on a baking sheet. Bake at 300° for 30 minutes or until lightly toasted. Remove pecans from oven and let cool. Store pecans in an airtight container. Yield: 4 cups.

Opposite: Plaid jar toppers tied with raffia bows, cinnamon sticks tucked into bright ribbon ties, decorative tins, and cross-stitched gift tags gussy up these easy gift ideas. (See page 44 for gift tag instructions.) Clockwise from front: Toasted Pecans on the Light Side, Spicy Pickled Pineapple, Christmas Brunch Jam.

Spicy Pickled Pineapple

3 (3-inch) sticks cinnamon, broken into 1-inch pieces
1 tablespoon whole cloves
1 tablespoon whole allspice
1 small lime, sliced
4 cups sugar
2 cups white wine vinegar (5% acidity)
2 large fresh pineapples, peeled, cored, and cut into 2- x 1/2- x 1/4-inch sticks

Tie cinnamon sticks, cloves, allspice, and lime in a cheesecloth bag and place it in a non-aluminum stockpot; add sugar and vinegar and bring to a boil, stirring frequently. Add pineapple; reduce heat and simmer 25 minutes or until pineapple is translucent, stirring occasionally. Remove and discard bag.

While the pineapple is still hot, pack it into hot, sterilized half-pint jars, leaving 1/2 inch of headspace. Cover pineapple with hot syrup, leaving 1/2 inch of headspace; wipe jar rims. Cover at once with metal lids and screw on bands. Process in a boiling water bath for 10 minutes. Yield: 9 half pints.

Christmas Brunch Jam

1 (20-ounce) can unsweetened pineapple tidbits, undrained
2 (6-ounce) jars red maraschino cherries, drained
2 (6-ounce) jars green maraschino cherries, drained
7 cups sugar
2 (3-ounce) packages liquid pectin

Drain pineapple, reserving 2 tablespoons juice. Cut cherries into quarters. Combine pineapple, reserved juice, cherries, and sugar in a large nonaluminum Dutch oven. Cook over medium-high heat, stirring constantly, until sugar dissolves. Bring mixture to a full, rolling boil and boil 1 minute. Stir in pectin and boil 1 minute. Remove from heat and skim off foam; let stand 10 minutes to slightly set jam and suspend fruit.

Ladle jam into hot, sterilized pint jars, leaving 1/4 inch of headspace; wipe jar rims. Cover at once with metal lids and screw on bands. Process in a boiling water bath 10 minutes. Yield: 4 pints.

Gift Tags That Keep on Giving

The name tags in the photograph on page 42 can be quickly cross-stitched on perforated paper. And these tags won't be thrown away after all the presents are opened. Tied with a bright ribbon and hung from the tree, they're sure to become cherished ornaments.

Materials:
charts and color key on page 136
4″ square perforated paper
embroidery floss (see color key)
embroidery needle
pinking shears
craft knife
⅓ yard (⅛″-wide) ribbon

Stitch design on 4″ square of perforated paper, following chart. Use alphabet to personalize within the borders. With pinking shears, trim paper on all sides, 3 holes from stitchery.

Follow the chart and use craft knife to cut away one small section of paper between 2 holes at top of gift tag. For hanger, thread ribbon through this opening.

Mocha Mix in an Instant

1½ cups instant nonfat dry milk powder
1½ cups powdered nondairy coffee
  creamer
1½ cups firmly packed brown sugar
¾ cup cocoa
¼ cup plus 2 tablespoons instant coffee
  granules
1⅔ cups miniature marshmallows

Combine dry milk powder, nondairy creamer, brown sugar, cocoa, and instant coffee, stirring well. Add marshmallows; toss lightly to combine. Yield: 7 cups.

Note: For each serving, spoon 3 tablespoons mix into a serving mug. Add 1 cup boiling water and stir well.

Store any leftover Mocha Mix, tightly covered, in a cool, dry place. The mix can become lumpy if exposed to moisture or high temperatures.

Opposite: For fancy gifts that are simple to make, seal our Mocha Mix in an Instant in a colorful glass jar, or make a few easy appliquéd gift bags to hold our Country Market Bean Soup Mix.

Country Market Bean Soup Mix

1 pound dried navy beans
1 pound dried pinto beans
1 pound dried Great Northern beans
1 pound dried green split peas
1 pound dried black-eyed peas
1 pound dried lentils
1 pound dried large limas
1 pound dried black beans
1 pound dried red kidney beans
1 pound barley pearls

Combine all ingredients, stirring well. Divide bean soup mix into 14 (1½-cup) portions. Place in 14 gift packages.

Note: Present mix with the following recipe for Country Market Bean Soup.

Country Market Bean Soup

1½ cups Country Market Bean Soup Mix
4 cups water
2 (10½-ounce) cans chicken broth,
  undiluted
½ teaspoon garlic powder
¼ teaspoon pepper
3 cups diced cooked ham
1 large onion, chopped
1 (16-ounce) can whole tomatoes,
  undrained and coarsely chopped
1 (4-ounce) can chopped green chilies,
  drained
3 tablespoons lime juice

Sort and wash 1½ cups Country Market Bean Soup Mix; place in a Dutch oven. Cover with water 2 inches above beans and soak overnight.

Drain off water, leaving beans in Dutch oven; add 4 cups water, undiluted chicken broth, garlic powder, and pepper. Cover and bring to a boil; reduce heat and simmer 1½ hours or until beans are tender. Add remaining ingredients and simmer, uncovered, 30 minutes, stirring occasionally. Serve hot. Yield: 2½ quarts.

Appliqué a Country Gift Bag

Combine bits of ribbon and lace with bright miniprints to make these colorful gift bags. The appliqué technique, using fusible web instead of stitches, makes them simple enough for even a novice crafter to make.

Ideas for using these delightful bags as gift presentations are practically endless. They're perfect as containers for our Country Market Bean Soup Mix (recipe on preceding page). Or pack them with your favorite holiday cookies or candy. Tie on a pretty recipe card for festive gifts, bazaar treasures, or Christmas party favors.

These gift wraps will be keepers. Stuffed with a bit of cotton or polyester stuffing, they'll make great tree-trimmers after the goodies are gone. Complete instructions are on the following page.

45

Gingerbread Man Bag

Materials:
pattern on page 136
¼ yard red cotton pindot fabric
⅓ yard (1″-wide) white gathered eyelet lace
white thread
scraps of brown cotton pindot fabric
scraps of paper-backed fusible web
18″ (⅛″-wide) green satin ribbon (for bows)
⅓ yard (¼″-wide) white rickrack
15″ (¹⁄₁₆″-wide) green satin ribbon
15″ (¹⁄₁₆″-wide) Prisma cellophane ribbon
needlepoint needle
10″ (¾″-wide) green/red/white striped
  grosgrain ribbon
3 (½″) gingerbread man buttons
white craft glue or hot-glue gun and glue
  sticks
2 (1½″-long) cinnamon sticks

Cut 9″ x 12″ rectangle from red fabric. Turn ¼″ to wrong side along one long edge and press. Stitch bound edge of eyelet along raw edge of ¼″ fold, with eyelet extending.

With wrong sides facing, fold fabric in half widthwise and press fold to crease. Open fabric and place right side up.

Following manufacturer's instructions, fuse web to wrong side of brown scraps. Transfer pattern to scraps and cut out. Using fold line as left edge of bag, fuse shapes to red fabric. (Refer to photograph on page 45 for placement.) Make 3 small bows from ⅛″-wide green ribbon and tack to necks of gingerbread men.

Machine-stitch rickrack on right side of red rectangle just below top fold.

With right sides facing, fold decorated bag along crease, aligning raw edges of side and bottom. Using ¼″ seam, stitch, leaving top open. Trim corners and turn.

Thread needle with ¹⁄₁₆″-wide satin and Prisma ribbons. Starting at right side seam, take running stitches around top of bag, just below rickrack. (Do not gather at this time.)

Tie a bow with grosgrain ribbon. Glue one button to center of bow. Tack bow to right side of bag, just above drawstring ribbons.

Fill bag with favorite Christmas goodies. Pull drawstrings to close bag and tie in a bow, leaving ends hanging. Thread one satin ribbon end through a cinnamon stick and then a button.

Knot ribbon end to secure. Trim excess, if desired. Repeat for other ribbon end. Lightly curl Prisma ribbon and allow to hang loosely.

Christmas Bell Bag

Materials:
pattern on page 136
¼ yard green cotton pindot fabric
⅓ yard (1″-wide) white gathered eyelet lace
white, red thread
scrap of paper-backed fusible web
scrap of red cotton miniprint
⅙ yard (½″-wide) green plaid ribbon
4″ (⅛″-wide) white rickrack
3 (¼″) gold jingle bells
⅓ yard (¼″-wide) white rickrack
⅓ yard (⅛″-wide) red rickrack
⅓ yard (1⅜″-wide) green plaid ribbon
white craft glue or hot-glue gun and glue
  sticks
15″ (¹⁄₁₆″-wide) red satin ribbon
15″ (¹⁄₁₆″-wide) Prisma cellophane ribbon
needlepoint needle
1 (3″) cinnamon stick

Make basic bag from green pindot fabric, using directions for Gingerbread Man Bag.

Following manufacturer's instructions, fuse web to wrong side of red scrap. Transfer pattern to scrap and cut out.

Fuse bell to right side of green fabric, referring to photograph for placement. Tie ½″-wide plaid ribbon in a bow and glue to top of bell. Cut ⅛″-wide piece of white rickrack in half and glue 2 rows across bell. Tack one jingle bell to bottom of fabric bell for clapper.

Machine-stitch ¼″-wide piece of white rickrack to right side of green rectangle just below top fold. Stitch narrow red rickrack along center of white rickrack.

Stitch bag seams, turn, and attach ribbons as directed for Gingerbread Man Bag.

Tie 1⅜″-wide plaid ribbon in a bow. Tack to right side of bag, just above drawstring ribbons.

Fill bag with favorite Christmas goodies and pull drawstrings to gather. Tie cinnamon stick to bag with ends of satin drawstring ribbon. Tie jingle bells to ends. Lightly curl Prisma ribbon and allow to hang loosely.

Above: Use a purchased apron and precut stencils to make a personalized Christmas gift for a special teacher or family member. Names can be added inside each heart with the aid of a red acrylic marker.

A Friendship Apron to Stencil

Looking for something special for your child to give her teacher this Christmas? Consider your own adaptation of the stenciled apron that Judy Ayscue, a first grade teacher at Matthew Whaley School in Williamsburg, Virginia, received from one of her students last year.

The project is a simple one. Rita Treleven, the mother of the student, started with a purchased apron. Then she bought the bear and heart stencils. (A wide selection of precut stencils is available at many craft and variety stores.)

With acrylic paint and a small stencil brush, Rita stenciled hearts around the apron's border and across the bib top. On the pocket, she stenciled the bears and heart. She tacked bows to the bears' necks and added the year to the heart with a red acrylic marker.

Each child in the class then signed his name inside one of the hearts, using the same red acrylic marker. Rita heat-set the paint by ironing the back of the apron.

The friendship apron idea can be expanded to become a gift for just about anyone on your Christmas list. Rita used the same design to fashion aprons as Christmas gifts for grandmothers and aunts in her family. (Don't forget grandfathers and uncles, too.)

And if you're looking for an auction or bazaar item to make, try this. Complete the apron, except for the names inside the hearts. Tuck a matching acrylic marker and instructions for completing the apron into the pocket. The purchaser can then use the apron as a gift for anyone she chooses.

A Calico Bear with Candy Treats

Even after the candy is gone, this little bear is sure to hold a lasting place in the hearts and holidays of the special friends on your Christmas list who receive him. He's surprisingly simple and inexpensive to make. So why not make several? But don't fill this bear's bag with just any candy. Pack his sack with our deliciously minty Malted-Sugar Taffy. (Recipe appears on the following page.)

Or use this whimsical candy holder as part of your own holiday decorations. Just be sure to make an extra supply of the taffy. You'll find it disappears so quickly that constant refills will be required throughout the season.

Materials for bear:
pattern on page 137
tracing paper
⅓ yard calico
black embroidery floss
embroidery needle
polyester stuffing
funnel or small spoon
¼ cup parakeet gravel or dry sand
7″ square of red felt
7½″ (1″-wide) eyelet trim
9″ (⅜″-wide) red ribbon

Transfer pattern pieces to tracing paper. Pin bear pattern to calico fabric and cut out front and back pieces.

Using 3 strands of black embroidery floss, embroider face. Use satin stitch for eyes and nose, backstitch for mouth.

With right sides facing, machine-stitch bear front and back, leaving opening in arm as indicated for turning and stuffing. Clip curves and turn. Loosely stuff ears with polyester stuffing. Machine- or hand-stitch on curved line dividing ears and head.

Using a funnel or spoon, fill one leg with gravel or sand. Pack by gently shaking leg until foot and leg are firmly filled. Hand- or machine-stitch on line dividing leg and body. Repeat for other leg.

Firmly stuff head, arms, and body with polyester stuffing. Hand-stitch opening closed.

Pin bag pattern to felt and cut out. Sew eyelet trim across upper edge of bag front, tucking under ½″ on each side.

Fold bag front on fold lines to form pleats and baste. With wrong sides facing, sew bag front to bag back along sides and bottom. Stitch edges of bag to bear's hands. Tie ribbon bow around bear's neck. Fill bag with candy.

Malted-Sugar Taffy

2 cups sugar
1 cup water
1 tablespoon malt vinegar
Red, green liquid food coloring
1 teaspoon peppermint extract

Combine sugar, water, and vinegar in a large saucepan, stirring well. Cook over medium heat, stirring constantly, until sugar dissolves. Cover and continue to cook 2 to 3 minutes to wash down sugar crystals from sides of pan. Uncover and cook, without stirring, until mixture reaches hard-ball stage (268°).

Remove from heat. Immediately pour half of the mixture into a lightly buttered saucepan and add red food coloring to reach desired tint, stirring until well blended. Tint the remaining mixture with green food coloring and stir until it is well blended.

Pour each portion of the candy onto a well-buttered baking sheet. Sprinkle evenly with peppermint extract and let cool to touch. Butter hands and pull each portion until light in color and difficult to pull. Pull each portion into a rope, ½ inch in diameter. Cut the ropes into 1-inch pieces and wrap in wax paper. Yield: about 8½ dozen.

Christmas Tree Bark

2 cups butter or margarine
2 cups sugar
2 tablespoons water
2 tablespoons light corn syrup
2 cups finely chopped pecans
6 ounces chocolate-flavored almond bark

Melt butter in a 4-quart Dutch oven over low heat. Add sugar, water, and corn syrup, stirring well. Bring to a boil, stirring constantly to dissolve sugar. Boil until mixture begins to lighten in color. Add pecans and continue to cook, stirring constantly, until mixture reaches soft-crack stage (285°).

Remove from heat and pour into a buttered 15- x 10- x 1-inch jellyroll pan, spreading the mixture to edges of pan. Let cool.

Place chocolate-flavored almond bark in top of a double boiler. Place over simmering water and cook, stirring frequently, until bark melts. Remove from heat and drizzle over candy. Let stand until bark is firm. Loosen edges of candy from pan, using a sharp knife; remove candy and break into coarse pieces to resemble tree bark. Store in an airtight container. Yield: about 3 pounds.

Note: Christmas Tree Bark may be presented for gift giving in festive baskets or tree-shaped glass containers.

5 Ideas

Festive Trims for Tasty Fare

Whether it's a basket of fruit, a bottle of wine, or homemade goodies from your kitchen, gifts of food make Christmas merrier. To make them even more special, here are some gift-wrap and presentation ideas.

Below: Create festive trims by wrapping paper doilies around miniature fruit tarts or boxes of your homemade candy.

Above: Place pieces of hard candy between two miniature paper doilies. Lace the doilies together with metallic cord or colorful ribbon for surprise-package stocking stuffers or holiday party favors.

Above: With a red marker or ballpoint pen, write your homemade bread recipe on a lacy white paper place mat. Wrap the place mat around your cellophane-covered loaf and top off the package with a Christmas bow and holly.

Right: Wind bright plaid and green grosgrain ribbons around a bottle of wine for a gift wrap that's simple but elegant.

Left: Embellish bottles of herbed or spiced vinegars and oils with bits of gold doilies, designs cut from old Christmas cards, wooden beads, or tiny Christmas bells.

Left: These wood-burned produce baskets are gifts in themselves. Fill them with fresh fruit, vegetables, or your homemade canned goods, and you'll have a special treat to give a special friend. To create your wood-burned basket, use one of the patterns on page 139 or a suitable design from a book or Christmas card. You might need to enlarge or reduce the pattern to fit the basket you have chosen. Your local photocopy store will do this for you for a small fee. Transfer the pattern to tracing paper and then to the basket, using carbon paper. With a very hot wood-burning tool, burn the solid lines first; then fill in letters with cross-hatching or dots.

The Coming of Santa Claus *by Thomas Nast*

Left and below: These gift bags, embellished with old-fashioned Victorian designs, are easy to make. The illustrations were photocopied onto 11" x 14" white paper. A second sheet was taped onto the first at the sides to form a tube, which was then folded and taped on the bottom. (See Diagram.) Books containing 19th-century wood engravings and line drawings are available at your bookstore, or see source listing on page 154.

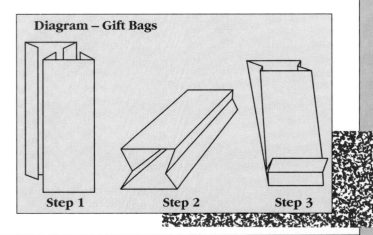

Diagram – Gift Bags

Step 1   Step 2   Step 3

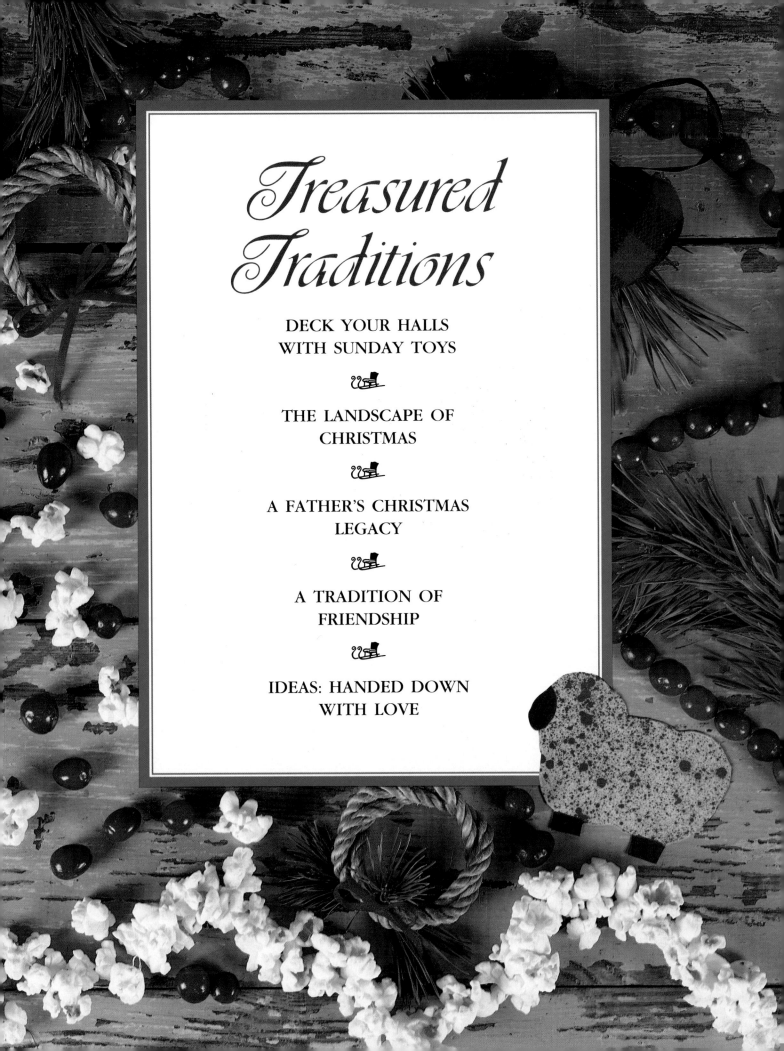

Treasured Traditions

DECK YOUR HALLS
WITH SUNDAY TOYS

THE LANDSCAPE OF
CHRISTMAS

A FATHER'S CHRISTMAS
LEGACY

A TRADITION OF
FRIENDSHIP

IDEAS: HANDED DOWN
WITH LOVE

Deck Your Halls With Sunday Toys

In many 19th-century homes, toys had to be put away on the Sabbath. Most Sunday play was frowned upon. Perhaps that's why toy Noah's arks gained such widespread popularity throughout America and Europe during that time. By playing with them, children were actually retelling the Bible story of the flood. So Victorian parents were more inclined to tolerate the presence of arks than of toy soldiers on a Sunday afternoon.

Today, Noah's arks are again in fashion, not as toys but as folk art collectibles. Because of their religious significance, they are especially favored during the holiday season and are often displayed with feather trees and folk art Santas.

Antique arks are rare and costly. But several excellent American folk artists create authentic-looking reproductions. Complete with Mr. and Mrs. Noah and crew, arks can be found in wood, tin, pewter, salt glaze pottery, papier-mâché, or almost any medium imaginable.

For more information about Noah's arks, see source listing on page 154.

Above: Like many of its original counterparts, this reproduction of a 19th-century German toy ark has a dove carrying an olive branch painted on its roof.

Right: Folk art patron Sherry Phillips's "keeping room" is a wonderland of whimsical treasures—especially at Christmastime. Dozens of Noah's arks, such as the two on the drop leaf table in the foreground, can be found here.

Right: This ark, designed by artist Gail Griffith, sits high and dry on its Chester County, Pennsylvania, mantel. A teddy bear named Little Muddy guards the animals lest they stray too far.

Left: Collector Barbara Hood of West Grove, Pennsylvania, had always wanted her own ark filled with friendly creatures, so she commissioned artist Elizabeth Pascko to make one. The artist has since moved to Australia, but Barbara is reminded of her friend every Christmas when she decorates a tabletop tree with lions, tigers, sheep, cats, and even kangaroos.

Right: Two by two, the beasts prepare to embark with Noah and his family. The ark and animals, created by Charlie Royston, are reproductions of a 19th-century set that the artist found in Indiana.

Above: A tiny Santa joins the animal passengers as they march toward a primitive-looking ark, where a pair of lanky lizards has already found the perfect place to travel. The miniature flags on the tree behind the ark are reproductions of flags that were waved at parades honoring returning union soldiers after the Civil War.

Left: Hand-carved animals make their way through a forest of garland greenery to the ark in the center. The Santa on the three-legged table is the work of a Wisconsin wood-carver.

Home-Baked Traditions from Around the World

Is there any more tantalizing aroma than that of hot bread, fresh from the oven — or any better time to add that aroma to the atmosphere of your home than at Christmastime?

This holiday season, you can introduce an international flavor to your bread baking with the following recipes. Try Italian Panettone, rich with fruit and nuts, or a braided Houska from Czechoslovakia. Serve up a Swiss Christmas breakfast with a sweet Saint Lucia's Coffee Cake Crown. Or keep your holiday strictly American with a mouth-watering Chocolate Yuletide Round spread with Mocha-Orange Frosting.

Chocolate Yuletide Rounds

4½ to 5 cups bread flour, divided
½ cup cocoa
1 cup sugar
2 packages dry yeast
1 teaspoon salt
¾ teaspoon ground cinnamon
¾ teaspoon ground nutmeg
½ teaspoon ground allspice
¾ cup water
½ cup milk
½ cup butter or margarine
3 eggs, beaten
¾ cup chopped pecans
½ cup coarsely chopped red candied cherries
½ cup coarsely chopped green candied cherries
Mocha-Orange Frosting (recipe follows)
Candied orange slices (optional)
Red and green candied cherries (optional)

Combine 2 cups flour, cocoa, sugar, yeast, salt, and spices in a large bowl, stirring well. Combine water, milk, and butter in a small saucepan; heat to 120° to 130°. Gradually add to flour mixture, beating well at low speed of an electric mixer. Add eggs and beat an additional 3 minutes at medium speed. Add pecans and coarsely chopped cherries, stirring to combine. Gradually stir in enough remaining flour to make a firm dough.

Turn dough out onto a floured surface and knead until smooth and elastic (about 8 to 10 minutes). Shape dough into a ball and place in a well-greased bowl, turning to grease top. Cover and let rise in a warm place (85°), free from drafts, 1½ hours or until doubled in bulk.

Punch dough down; turn out onto floured surface and knead lightly 4 or 5 times. Divide dough in half and shape each into a round loaf. Place each loaf in a greased 8-inch springform pan; gently press top of each loaf to flatten and conform loaf to pan. Cover and let rise in a warm place (85°), free from drafts, 1½ hours or until doubled in bulk. Bake at 350° for 35 to 40 minutes or until loaves sound hollow when tapped. Loosen sides of springform pans; remove loaves from pans and transfer to wire racks to cool completely.

Spread Mocha-Orange Frosting evenly over top of each loaf, allowing excess to drizzle down sides. If desired, attractively arrange candied orange slices and cherries on top of each loaf. Yield: 2 loaves.

Mocha-Orange Frosting:

1½ cups semisweet chocolate morsels
3 tablespoons butter or margarine
1½ cups sifted powdered sugar
3 tablespoons Kahlùa or other coffee-flavored liqueur
1 tablespoon plus 1½ teaspoons orange juice

Combine chocolate morsels and butter in top of a double boiler. Place over simmering water and cook, stirring frequently, until chocolate melts. Remove from heat and let cool. Add powdered sugar, liqueur, and orange juice; beat at medium speed of an electric mixer until well blended. Use immediately. Yield: about 1½ cups.

Opposite: The heritage of many Americans is represented in this table full of hearty holiday breads. Clockwise from top left: Saint Lucia's Coffee Cake Crown, Houska, Chocolate Yuletide Round, Panettone.

Panettone

5 to 5½ cups all-purpose
 flour, divided
½ cup sugar
2 packages dry yeast
1½ teaspoons anise seeds
1 teaspoon salt
1¼ cups milk
¼ cup water
½ cup butter or margarine
2 eggs, beaten
1 teaspoon vanilla extract
½ cup golden raisins
½ cup chopped almonds
⅓ cup mixed chopped candied
 fruit
1 egg
1 tablespoon milk

Combine 3 cups flour, sugar, yeast, anise
seeds, and salt in a large bowl, stirring until well
blended. Set flour mixture aside.

Combine 1¼ cups milk, water, and butter in a
small saucepan; heat to 120° to 130°. Gradually
add hot milk mixture to flour mixture, beating
well at low speed of an electric mixer. Add
beaten eggs and vanilla extract; beat an additional 2 minutes at medium speed. Add raisins,
almonds, and candied fruit, stirring until well
blended. Gradually stir in enough remaining
flour to make a soft dough.

Turn dough out onto a floured surface and
knead until smooth and elastic (about 8 to 10
minutes). Shape dough into a ball and place in a
well-greased bowl, turning to grease top. Cover
and let rise in a warm place (85°), free from
drafts, 1 hour or until doubled in bulk.

Punch dough down; turn out onto floured surface and knead lightly 4 or 5 times. Divide
dough into 3 equal portions; shape each into a
round loaf. Place loaves on lightly greased baking sheets. Cover and let rise in a warm place
(85°), free from drafts, 30 minutes or until doubled in bulk.

Combine egg and 1 tablespoon milk, beating
with a fork until well blended; gently brush over
loaves.

Bake at 350° for 20 to 25 minutes or until the
loaves are golden brown and sound hollow
when tapped. Transfer to wire racks to cool.
Yield: 3 loaves.

Houska

1 package dry yeast
½ cup plus 1 teaspoon sugar, divided
¼ cup warm water (105° to 115°)
4½ to 5½ cups all-purpose flour, divided
2 teaspoons salt
1 teaspoon grated orange rind
¼ teaspoon ground mace
1 cup milk
¼ cup butter or margarine
3 eggs, beaten
1 cup raisins
½ cup finely chopped walnuts
1 egg
1 tablespoon milk

Dissolve yeast and 1 teaspoon sugar in warm
water; let stand 5 minutes.

Combine 4½ cups flour, remaining ½ cup
sugar, salt, orange rind, and mace in a large
bowl, stirring well. Make a well in center of
mixture. Combine milk and butter in a small
saucepan; heat to 105° to 115°. Add beaten eggs,
yeast mixture, and milk mixture to flour mixture, beating well at medium speed of a heavy-
duty electric mixer.

Turn dough out onto a floured surface; add
raisins and walnuts. Knead until smooth and
elastic (about 8 to 10 minutes), incorporating
raisins and walnuts and adding remaining flour
as needed to make a soft dough. Shape dough
into a ball and place in a well-greased bowl,
turning to grease top. Cover and let rise in a
warm place (85°), free from drafts, 1 hour or
until doubled in bulk.

Punch dough down; turn out onto floured surface and knead lightly 4 or 5 times. Divide
dough into 5 equal portions; shape each into an
18-inch rope. Place 3 ropes side by side on a
lightly greased baking sheet; braid ropes and
tuck ends under to seal. Twist remaining 2
ropes and place lengthwise on top of braid,
tucking ends under to seal. Cover and let rise in
a warm place (85°), free from drafts, 30 to 45
minutes or until doubled in bulk.

Combine egg and milk, beating with a fork
until well blended; gently brush mixture over
braided loaf. Bake at 325° for 35 minutes or
until loaf is golden brown and sounds hollow
when tapped. Transfer loaf to a wire rack to
cool. Yield: 1 loaf.

Saint Lucia's Coffee Cake Crown

3 to 3½ cups all-purpose flour, divided
¼ cup sugar
1 package dry yeast
1 teaspoon salt
⅛ teaspoon ground saffron
½ cup milk
¼ cup plus 2 tablespoons water
2 tablespoons butter or margarine
1 egg
½ cup chopped pecans
½ cup chopped candied pineapple
3 tablespoons chopped candied lemon peel
1½ cups sifted powdered sugar
3 tablespoons milk
Lemon zest (optional)

Combine 1½ cups flour, ¼ cup sugar, yeast, salt, and saffron in a large bowl, stirring until well blended. Set flour mixture aside.

Combine milk, water, and butter in a small saucepan; heat to 120° to 130°. Gradually add hot milk mixture to flour mixture, beating well at medium speed of an electric mixer. Continue to beat 2 minutes. Add egg and ½ cup flour; beat an additional 2 minutes at high speed. Add pecans and candied fruit, stirring to combine. Gradually stir in enough remaining flour to make a soft dough.

Turn dough out onto a floured surface and knead until smooth and elastic (about 8 to 10 minutes). Cover and let rest 20 minutes. Divide dough into 3 equal portions; shape each into a 23-inch rope.

Place ropes side by side on a lightly greased baking sheet; braid ropes. Shape braid into a circle, pinching ends to seal. Cover and let rise in a warm place (85°), free from drafts, 1 hour or until doubled in bulk. Bake at 375° for 20 to 25 minutes or until loaf is golden brown and sounds hollow when tapped. Transfer to a wire rack to cool completely.

Combine powdered sugar and milk, beating with a wire whisk until smooth; drizzle over braided loaf. Garnish top of loaf with lemon zest, if desired. Yield: 1 loaf.

Right: This beautiful table quilt, bright with holly leaves and berries, will help you dress your home for a country Christmas.

Holly Leaf Table Cover

No matter what holiday fare your table holds, it deserves to be dressed for the season. And these holly leaves and berries will dress your table in fine country style.

Materials:
pattern on pages 140-141
cardboard or plastic template material
3⅜ yards (45"-wide) muslin
⅛ yard (45"-wide) green fabric
¾ yard (45"-wide) red fabric
**½ yard (45"-wide) Christmas print with
    white background**
**1 yard (45"-wide) red fabric for binding (or
    purchased red bias binding)**
57" square of batting
red, green thread
off-white quilting thread
quilting needle

Note: All seam allowances are ¼". Press seams toward darker fabric.

Extend pattern pieces and transfer to template material. Remove selvages from muslin. Fold

muslin in half across the width of the fabric. Cut along fold.

With right sides facing, machine-stitch the 2 pieces of muslin together along one long edge to form one piece of muslin. Press seam open.

From the outer edges of this large piece of muslin, cut 2 pieces, 10½" x 12½" (piece G), and one piece, 32½" x 12½" (piece H). From Christmas print, cut 4 squares, 8½" (piece C). Cut remaining pieces as indicated on pattern.

Using matching thread, baste and then appliqué holly leaves and berries to squares and triangles, as indicated in Diagram.

Using matching thread, sew 2 pieces A and then 2 pieces B to one piece C to form corner square. (See Diagram.) Repeat 3 times for 4 corner squares. Press seams.

Sew one piece F to one side of one piece G. Repeat with one more F and G. Press seams. Sew a piece F to each end of piece H. Press seams. Sew 2 pieces D to a piece E. Repeat 3 times for 4 triangles. Press seams.

Referring to Diagram for placement, sew a corner square unit to each end of both F-G squares to form 2 rows. Sew these rows to each side of the long (H-F) strip to form a large square. Press seams.

Center and sew E-D triangles in place. (See Diagram.) Press seams.

Mark quilting lines ¼" inside all seams, except piece G-H joining seams. Mark a 2" grid on piece G-H. (See Diagram.)

Lay remaining muslin (for backing) wrong side up. Place batting on muslin. Center quilt top, right side up, on batting. Baste or pin with safety pins. Trim excess muslin and batting even with quilt top edge.

Following quilting lines, stitch through all layers, using off-white quilting thread. With red thread, outline-quilt ⅛" from edges of leaves and berries. Quilt center veins of leaves in red.

Bind edges of table cover with a 2" continuous bias strip of red fabric or with purchased red bias binding.

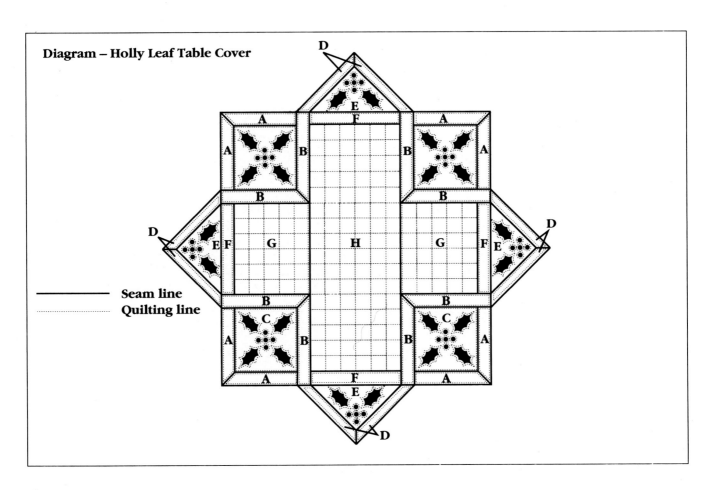

Diagram – Holly Leaf Table Cover

——— Seam line
········· Quilting line

Simple Sheep with An Old-World Appeal

Benel's sheep were wonderful to behold! They were shaped out of clay, then cotton was wrapped around them, four matches were stuck in to represent legs, and a splash of Chinese vermillion was daubed on the end where the nose belonged.
—from *A Century of Moravian Sisters*
   by E. L. Myers (Copyright 1918)

The picture of Moravian sisters painting with Chinese vermillion may be exotic, but Sister Benel's little sheep were the height of simplicity. Benel was a Moravian seamstress who lived and worked in Bethlehem, Pennsylvania, early in the century. Her petite sheep were especially prized for their use in the miniature landscapes—the *putzes*—the Moravians traditionally built at Christmas. (For more information, see the *putz* on the following pages.) Variations of Benel's sheep are still being made in the area today.

Begin your own tradition by shaping a flock to graze near your manger this Christmas.

Materials for two sheep:
1 small package Sculpey III modeling
   compound in off-white
8 small wooden matchsticks (burn or
   remove heads)
craft glue
absorbent cotton or cotton batting
acrylic paints: red, black
toothpick or fine artists' brush
scrap of ribbon or embroidery floss

For sheep's body, work Sculpey with hands until soft and pliable. Form into 3″ roll. Bend one end up to form neck and head. Gently shape face. Roll another piece of Sculpey to size of small pea. Stretch and flatten to form 1″ long flat oval. Lay over top of head and smooth to form ears.

Insert 4 matchsticks into body for legs. Set on flat surface to make sure sheep stands evenly. Adjust legs as needed.

Bake or harden according to manufacturer's instructions. Longer baking will make sheep darker. Although sheep shown are white, they may be painted black for Shropshire effect, after cooling.

To form wool, lightly cover body area with glue. Stretch a piece of cotton into a long, thin strip. Wrap cotton around sheep body. Pull it tightly; then release it, allowing it to expand and look more wool-like. Continue wrapping and re-leasing cotton until sheep looks woolly enough.

Paint 2 black dots for eyes and a red dot for nose, referring to photograph as a guide.

Tie ribbon or floss around neck for a bow.

The Landscape of Christmas

All over America there's a bustling to search for "the perfect tree." Families carry ornaments down from the attic and decorate their trees in traditional ways. The Christmas tree brings a piece of the landscape inside for the season. For the Moravians, a Protestant denomination established in the colonies in the 1740s, that tradition goes a step further. They create an entire landscape, called a *putz* (pùts).

From the German word *putzen*, meaning to decorate, a *putz* is a child's dream-come-true manger scene. It includes scores of figures and animals in a miniature landscape showing the story of the Nativity.

Every year around Thanksgiving, Dr. Robert Knouss finds a way to get back to his parents' home in Bethlehem, Pennsylvania. Bethlehem, one of the first Moravian settlements, received its name in a Christmas Eve vigil service in

Above: "And, lo, the angel of the Lord came upon them, and the glory of the Lord shone round about them: and they were sore afraid."

—from The Gospel according to Luke

1741 by Count Zinzendorf, benefactor and spiritual leader of the Pennsylvania Moravians. Now the Bethlehem in Pennsylvania is known as the Christmas City, with tours coming from around the world to see Moravian *putzes* from Thanksgiving to New Year's Eve.

As deputy director of the Pan-American Health Organization, Robert travels great distances some holidays to return to Bethlehem. His own family travels with him to continue a tradition that began for him and his parents, Alice and Francis Knouss, many holidays ago.

"When Robert was in kindergarten he got out a card table and set up a Nativity scene," says Mrs. Knouss. That simple act started a tradition that has grown to fill an entire room of their home.

"A neighbor got him interested and then gave him his first crèche figures," says Mrs. Knouss.

Those first plaster figurines, while beautiful, are no match for today's collection. Every figure in the Knousses' *putz* is hand-carved and painted by the German wood-carver, Ludwig Krauss of Oberammergau. The figures have a touch of artistry that very nearly breathes spirit into Mary, Joseph, and the little babe.

These finely carved figures alone would be intriguing, but Robert adds his own artistry. First, he constructs a base for the *putz*. He arranges boxes of various shapes and heights and then forms newspaper around them to produce different levels. Fresh moss gathered in the Poconos covers the top of the construction. Driftwood and tree stumps, passed down from generations of Moravian families around Bethlehem, are carefully placed to make room for scenes of the Christmas story. Lights are installed at this time, so that each scene can be illuminated separately.

"Forty or 50 years ago, we would go *putzing.* People would have open house through the Christmas season to share their *putzes* with the community," Mrs. Knouss says. Each Moravian family had an individual style. One *putz* would lie under the tree; another would rest on a tabletop. Barnyard animals filled one; a small lake with swans graced another.

"A *putz* is not just the Nativity story, but your own Christmas story," Mrs. Knouss says. "It's just not Christmas until the *putz* is in place."

Start a Star-Bright Tradition

The star has been associated with Christmas since the Star of the East guided the three Wise Men on their long journey to the manger. A symbol of the light of the world, the star continues to brighten our holidays today.

Colonial Coverlet Ornaments, Sweet Gum Stars, Beeswax Ornaments, and Two-Color Paper Stars are all traditional ornaments that can shine on a theme tree or bring a new sparkle to your collection of older treasures.

Colonial Coverlet Ornaments

Materials:
worn fragments of overshot coverlet or
   purchased place mat with overshot
   pattern
medium- to heavyweight iron-on interfacing
white glue
string or ribbon for hanger
liquid ravel preventer

Note: Overshot is one of the earliest coverlet weaves. Dark threads lie on the light-colored warp, skipping a number of threads; hence the name overshot or float weave. Handwoven place mats like the ones used for these ornaments can be ordered. See source listing on page 154.

Back wrong side of fabric with iron-on interfacing. Carefully cut out 2 matching overshot designs. Coat wrong side of one design with a thin, even layer of white glue. Make hanging loop and lay ends on back of one star. Place designs wrong sides facing, matching edges. Press layers firmly together and allow to dry. Apply liquid ravel preventer to edges. Let dry.

Opposite: With this shimmering collection of star ornaments, your tree will be aglow. Simple sweet gum seed balls seem to burst with light. A modest paper chain crafted of gold foil adds even more sparkle. Colonial Coverlet Ornaments give the tree the brightness of Christmas red.

Sweet Gum Stars

Materials:
sweet gum tree seed balls
toothpicks
thick white craft glue
spray paint in desired color

Apply small amount of craft glue to one end of a toothpick and insert in a hole of the sweet gum ball. Repeat to fill every hole. Let dry. Paint as desired.

To vary size of stars, cut 1" or 2" from one end of each toothpick. Glue cut end into ball.

Place these stars on top of tree branches. Or loop sewing thread around the sweet gum ball, making a swing to hang the star.

Beeswax Ornaments

Materials:
100% beeswax (paraffin is not
   recommended)
old double boiler
metal tart tins or small plastic, heat-resistant
   cookie molds
short pieces of cotton string
toothpick
1/16"-wide satin ribbon

Note: Contact your county agricultural agent or a health food store for help in locating a local beekeeper who will sell you wax. Or check with craft shops for availability of pure beeswax. The double boiler can be improvised by using a clean tin can and an old cooking pot.

Chip wax and place in top of double boiler. Melt over water on medium heat. (Never heat wax over direct source of heat or at higher than medium heat, because wax may ignite. Replace water in bottom of double boiler as it boils away. Do not leave unattended.)

When wax has liquefied, pour carefully into clean, dry molds, filling to just below rim. Cut a 1" length of string and fold it in half to form loop. Using a toothpick, submerge ends of string in the hot wax near top of mold. Cool molds in refrigerator or freezer until wax is hard.

To unmold, dip mold briefly up to rim in cool water, rap back of mold with spoon, and invert mold. Wax should pop right out. (If wax cracks or surface is imperfect, simply melt and mold again.) Tie a 6″ length of ribbon to string loop for hanger.

To store, pack flat in single layers. Separate layers with cardboard. Store in cool, dry place to prevent melting during summer heat.

Two-Color Paper Stars

Materials for two stars:
craft glue
4″ x 16″ sheet of red wrapping paper
4″ x 16″ sheet of green wrapping paper
craft knife
metal ruler
toothpick or fingernail file
paraffin
florists' wire
thin gold cord

Note: Variations of this folded star have been around since the 1800s. The directions may seem complicated at first, but if you follow each step carefully, the diagrams will guide you through. Make a trial star first; the second one will be much easier.

Thin craft glue with a little water and brush evenly on back of one sheet of wrapping paper. Bond the 2 sheets together with wrong sides facing and allow to dry.

Using the craft knife and metal ruler, cut 4 (½″ x 16″) strips from this sheet. (It is important to cut these strips accurately so that they weave properly.) Fold each strip in half widthwise so that the same color is on the outside. Trim ends to a point. Loop all 4 strips into a basket weave. (See Diagram 1.) Pull tight.

Starting with top left, fold down only the top strip. (See Diagram 2.) Turning piece clockwise, fold down each of the 3 remaining strips as they move to top left. After folding down the final one, weave it under bottom left square. (See Diagram 3.)

Starting with top right strip, fold strip to the right at a 45° angle. (See Diagram 4.) Then fold strip forward and down to make a triangle. (See Diagram 5.) Fold the triangle in half (see Diagram 6), and weave end of strip under top right square. Turn piece clockwise and repeat the steps shown in Diagrams 4, 5, and 6 to make points on 3 remaining short strips. Flip the star over. Starting with top right strip, repeat the above procedure, referring again to Diagrams 4, 5, and 6 to make 4 remaining outer points. (Note that red and green are reversed on the opposite side. See Diagram 7.)

To make inner points, flip the long right strip out of the way to the left. (See Diagram 8.) Pick up bottom right strip and, keeping top side up, loop it to right as shown. Insert tip of looped strip into top left square of basketweave and push it through, so that it comes through the folded point on the top left side of the star. (To make weaving easier, insert toothpick or fingernail file through the opening in the folded point to widen the slot and help guide the paper strip.) Gently pull strip through to form a cone.

68

Two-Color Paper Stars

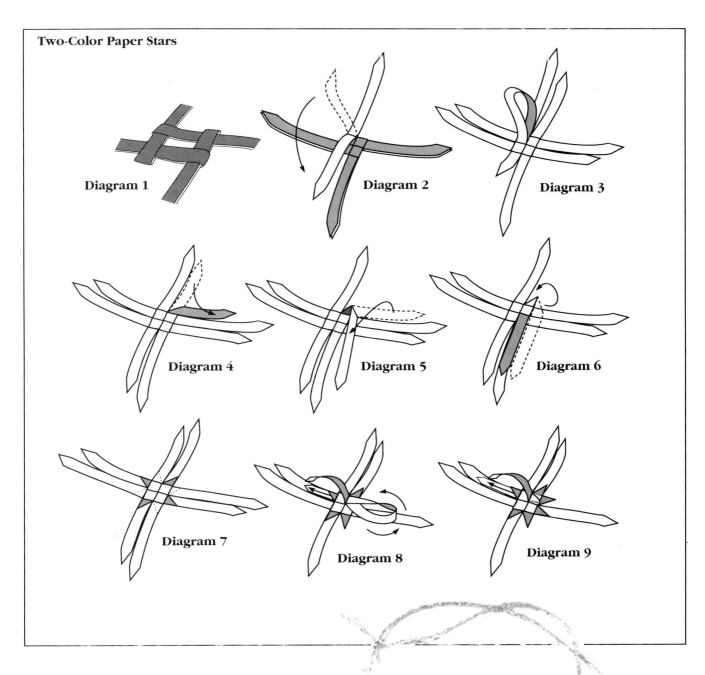

Diagram 1

Diagram 2

Diagram 3

Diagram 4

Diagram 5

Diagram 6

Diagram 7

Diagram 8

Diagram 9

(See Diagram 9.) Turn star clockwise and repeat to make 3 more inner points. Flip star over and repeat, starting with bottom right strip, to make 4 remaining inner points.

Trim loose strands off even with points of star. Dip completed star in melted paraffin to protect it. Thread a length of florists' wire through star to use as a handle. (If too much wax collects on star, dip quickly in hot water to remove excess wax.) Allow to dry; then remove wire. Thread a piece of cord through hole for ornament hanger.

A Father's Christmas Legacy

Carol hugs a precious Christmas gift, a teddy bear that her father made more than 40 years ago.

The Christmas when Carol Boyer was two years old, her father, who was in the service, sent home a big stuffed teddy bear that he had made. Illness had put him in a field hospital in Texas, and various activities were offered to help recuperating servicemen pass the time. Carol's father learned to sew. In later years, he added knitting, crochet, and upholstering to his skills as well.

Carol says, "My father always loved to work with his hands. When he was 13, he traced patterns from his mother's quilt book and pieced them together. I still have the blocks."

Carol's father died a couple of years ago, leaving his family many handmade heirlooms, which keep his memory close. More than 40 years old now, the Christmas bear is one of Carol's most prized possessions. But it is only one of many presents her father made for her.

Carol's desire to display and use her father's crafts led her to the warm country look in decorating. And relatives and friends added to her country collection. When it came time to build a new house, Carol's husband, Dee, who is a contractor, added architectural elements—such as pine boards for crown moldings and door frames—to give their new home in Virginia a distinct country style, and create the perfect setting for all their keepsakes.

Top: Carol mentioned to a friend that she wanted to find a sweater for her bear. Knowing how special the stuffed toy was to Carol, her friend gave her a baby sweater crocheted by the friend's mother for the mother's first grandchild.

Carol's father crocheted the dining room table mats after Carol showed him a picture of some similar mats that she liked. Carol says, "When I was growing up, I would show my father magazine photos of sweaters, scarves, and other things I liked, and he would knit or crochet them for me. He didn't even need directions."

Left: The Boyers' living room is decorated with gifts from family and friends. On the coffee table, which is an old oak library table that Dee cut down, are an antique tool box filled with apples, cones, and greenery, and a box made by a neighbor, holding gingerbread men nestled in a tea towel. The rag balls were made by Carol by wrapping torn strips around craft-foam balls.

Carol's father made the ribbon-laced afghan on the sofa for his granddaughter Jenny. Jenny made the checked latchhook pillow for Carol. The big white bear, a gift to Jenny, has a sentimental origin. It was made from a coat that Dee gave Carol on their first Christmas together. Carol found the other teddies, which are made from recycled blankets and coats, while visiting her mom in Pennsylvania.

Carol made the cross-stitched piece on the wall, and the wreath of cones was made by a friend. The shelf and the wooden gingerbread men were crafted by a cousin's teenage son. The fresh greenery on the shelf and throughout the house is from Pennsylvania. Carol explains, "We bring back big sacks of blue spruce every year when we go home for Thanksgiving."

Above: These crocheted stockings, suspended from an antique bed rail, hold sweet memories. Years ago after undergoing back surgery, Carol faced weeks of convalescence. Her father showed her how to make a granny square, a traditional building block of crochet, and suggested that she make a stocking. Carol had problems starting squares, a tricky step for beginners, so her father did the centers and Carol finished the squares.

71

Hearty Northwest Christmas Breakfast

Buckwheat Flapjacks
with Blueberry-Lemon Syrup
Smoked Salmon Omelets
Idaho Hash Browns
Northwest Eye-Opener
Hot Coffee
(Menu serves 4.)

Snow's piled high, almost touching the windows. The first fire of the morning warms the kitchen. Guests will arrive soon, and you're prepared for the biggest of appetites.

Hash browns topped with cheese and cracked pepper nestle in beside Smoked Salmon Omelets. The omelets brim over with tomato, fresh dill, and, of course, that king of the Northwest—salmon. Buckwheat Flapjacks, dripping with Blueberry-Lemon Syrup, are the crowning touch.

It's a feast fit for a lumberjack, so why not cover your dining table with a robust red-and-black buffalo plaid? Complete the look with matching heart-shaped napkin holders. Your guests can take them home as a memento of a wholesome Christmas-morning banquet.

Buckwheat Flapjacks with Blueberry-Lemon Syrup

½ cup buckwheat flour
½ cup all-purpose flour
1 teaspoon baking powder
½ teaspoon baking soda
½ teaspoon salt
1 cup plus 2 tablespoons buttermilk
1 egg, beaten
2 tablespoons butter or margarine, melted
1 teaspoon molasses
Blueberry-Lemon Syrup (recipe follows)

Combine first 5 ingredients in a medium bowl, stirring well. Combine buttermilk, egg,

butter, and molasses; add to dry ingredients, stirring just until moistened.

For each flapjack, spoon 2 tablespoons batter onto a hot, lightly greased griddle. Turn flapjacks when the tops are covered with bubbles and the edges look cooked. Serve immediately with Blueberry-Lemon Syrup. Yield: 12 (4-inch) flapjacks.

Blueberry-Lemon Syrup:

2 cups frozen blueberries
¼ cup plus 2 tablespoons water, divided
¼ cup frozen lemonade concentrate,
   thawed and undiluted
2 tablespoons sugar
1 tablespoon cornstarch

Combine frozen blueberries, ¼ cup water, lemonade concentrate, and sugar in a small, heavy saucepan; bring to a boil. Reduce heat and simmer 3 minutes or until blueberries pop. Dissolve cornstarch in remaining 2 tablespoons water; stir into blueberry mixture and return to a boil. Boil 1 minute or until mixture thickens, stirring constantly. Remove from heat and serve warm or at room temperature over flapjacks or waffles. Store syrup in refrigerator in an airtight container. Yield: 1½ cups.

Westward Bound!

Pancakes became a favorite breakfast staple as settlers moved West. Made from readily available ingredients, stacks of these griddle or pancakes provided a quick and substantial meal for hardworking men and women.

For the best pancakes today, remember that beating the batter results in tough pancakes. To make light, fluffy pancakes, mix the ingredients only until they are moistened.

Opposite: When you finish this breakfast, you'll feel as happy as the bright-eyed squirrels in the centerpiece. Instructions for the Buffalo Plaid Napkin Rings can be found on page 74.

Smoked Salmon Omelets

1 cup sliced fresh mushrooms
½ cup coarsely chopped green onions
2 tablespoons butter or margarine, melted
⅔ cup Chablis or other dry white wine
½ pound smoked salmon, coarsely chopped
⅔ cup coarsely chopped, peeled tomato
¼ cup chopped fresh dillweed
1½ teaspoons lemon juice
½ teaspoon salt
¼ teaspoon white pepper
2 tablespoons butter or margarine, divided
8 eggs
¼ cup milk

Sauté mushrooms and onions in 2 tablespoons butter in a medium skillet until tender. Add wine; cook over medium heat until liquid is absorbed. Stir in salmon and next 5 ingredients; cook, stirring frequently, until thoroughly heated. Remove from heat; keep warm.

Heat a 10-inch omelet pan or heavy skillet over medium heat until hot enough to sizzle a drop of water. Add 1 tablespoon butter and rotate pan to coat bottom. Combine eggs and milk; stir well. Pour half of egg mixture into pan; set remaining egg mixture aside. As mixture starts to cook, gently lift edges of omelet with a spatula and tilt pan so uncooked portion flows underneath. When egg mixture is set, spoon half of salmon mixture over half of omelet; set remaining salmon mixture aside.

Loosen omelet with a spatula; fold in half and slide onto serving platter. Repeat cooking process with remaining butter, egg, and salmon mixture. Cut each omelet in half and serve immediately. Yield: 4 servings.

Idaho Hash Browns

4 medium potatoes (about 1¾ pounds)
⅓ cup bacon drippings
⅓ cup coarsely chopped onion
⅓ cup coarsely chopped green pepper
⅓ cup coarsely chopped sweet red pepper
1 clove garlic, minced
2 tablespoons grated Parmesan cheese
2 tablespoons minced fresh parsley
½ teaspoon salt
¼ teaspoon cracked pepper

Place potatoes in a medium saucepan; add water to cover. Bring to a boil and cook 15 minutes or until tender. Drain and let cool slightly. Peel potatoes and cut into ½-inch cubes; set aside.

Melt bacon drippings in a large skillet over low heat. Add potatoes and cook over medium-high heat, stirring frequently, until browned. Add onion, chopped peppers, and garlic. Continue to cook, stirring frequently, 2 to 3 minutes or until vegetables are tender. Gently stir in cheese and remaining ingredients. Remove from heat and serve hot. Yield: 4 servings.

Northwest Eye-Opener

1 (6-ounce) can frozen grapefruit juice concentrate, thawed and undiluted
½ cup frozen lemonade concentrate, thawed and undiluted
½ cup orange juice
3 tablespoons grenadine syrup
1 (33.8-ounce) bottle ginger ale, chilled
Crushed ice
Red maraschino cherries with stems (optional)

Combine first 4 ingredients in a medium-size pitcher. Cover and refrigerate until thoroughly chilled. Stir in ginger ale and pour over crushed ice just before serving. If desired, garnish with cherries. Yield: 1½ quarts.

Buffalo Plaid Napkin Rings

Materials for one napkin ring:
pattern on page 141
scraps of buffalo plaid fabric or other woolen check
stuffing
9½" (¼"-wide) black satin ribbon
thread to match

Transfer pattern to fabric and cut out. With right sides facing, stitch fabric hearts together, using ¼" seam and leaving open where indicated. Turn and stuff. Slipstitch opening closed.

To make loop, fold ribbon in half and tie ends together in a square knot 1" from tips. Slipstitch knot to center top of heart.

Sponge and Spatter These Folk Art Ornaments

In colonial America, faux-finish techniques were used to give walls, floors, and furniture the look of expensive materials such as marble, granite, or hardwood. We have used two of these techniques, sponge and spatter painting, to produce folksy animals that are perfect for tree or package ornaments.

Materials:
patterns on page 139
sheet of oaktag or manila file folders
acrylic paints: black, brown, green, red (or colors of choice)
paper plates
small sponges
toothbrushes
small paintbrushes
tung oil varnish
soft cloth
small amount of coarse rope (for horse)
craft glue (for horse)
scrap of ⅛" satin ribbon (for rabbit)
gold thread (for hangers)

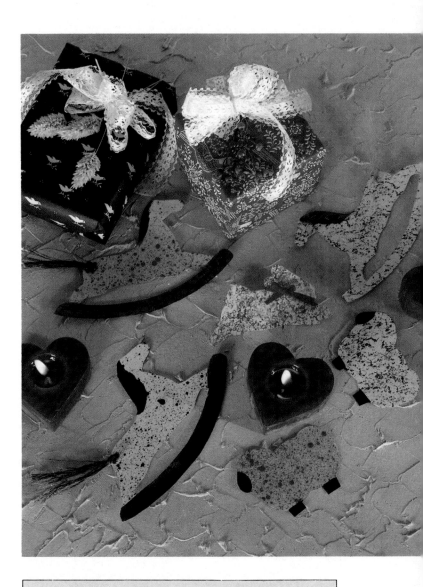

Transfer patterns to oaktag and cut out. To sponge-paint, dip a damp sponge in a few drops of paint on paper plate. Dab paint lightly on cut-out shapes. To spatter-paint, place shapes on newspaper. Dip bristles of toothbrush into paint. Draw your finger over the bristles and spatter paint onto shapes.

Using paintbrush, paint horse's mane and rocker and sheep's face and feet black. Let dry completely. Using cloth, rub 3 coats of varnish on each side of shapes, allowing to dry between coats.

For horse's tail, tie a knot at one end of a 4" length of rope. Separate the strands and paint a few of them with black paint, if desired. Glue the knot to the horse.

For rabbit, tie ribbon around neck in a bow. For hanger, thread a needle with a 5" length of gold thread. Punch needle through shape where indicated. Knot thread ends together.

Try These Techniques, Too

Comb painting: Paint surface and allow to dry thoroughly. Then apply a second color. While still wet, drag a comb through paint.

Rag painting: Dab freshly painted surface with wadded cloth—burlap, cheesecloth, etc.

Feather painting: While paint is wet, drag a feather across surface.

A Tradition of Friendship

On a cold December morning on a hill in East Tennessee, cars and vans quickly fill the driveway at June Redmond's home. Snow flurries ride the brisk wind as ladies emerge from their automobiles. Dull clouds tease with the promise of a white Christmas, while visitors rush to the warmth of June's country kitchen and a cup of steaming hot cider.

They have come for June's annual "Saturday Morning with Friends," a Christmas tradition begun several years ago and always observed on the Saturday morning before Christmas.

"The ladies just drop by," explains June. "Some are in jogging suits on their way to the grocery or to pick up their children. Others are all dressed up for a party because this is one of their special occasions."

"It's become a tradition that we anticipate," adds Alice McWilliams, one of June's longtime friends. "It's our time to stop and be thankful for close friends during the usual hustle and bustle of the season."

"Friends give special meaning to Christmas," adds June. "We should always remember to give thanks for the gift of good friends."

June designs an original invitation each year for her holiday gathering. She also makes each guest a new ornament as a remembrance of the day. Last year, the ornament was a painted wooden heart, tied with a red ribbon for hanging and presented in a pretty paper bag decorated with country hearts and holly. Some years, her handmade gifts adorn a special tree from which guests make their selections. And, of course, her guests also bring handmade and home-baked gifts to pass around.

Emphasizing tradition is a way of life for June and Alice and their friend Bonnie Sheeley. Many of their observances involve the three of them and their other friends: such as the Christmas brunch, their Thursday-night get-togethers, or the "We Three" mini-vacations that June, Bonnie, and Alice take frequently. But they believe that traditions are especially valuable for families, too.

For instance, their children have ornament boxes to which a new ornament is added each

Above: They call themselves "We Three," and they believe that a friend is one of the blessings of life, to be remembered in a special way at Christmas. Standing, June Redmond; seated, from left, Alice McWilliams and Bonnie Sheeley.

Above: On the Saturday morning before Christmas, friendships are renewed with good food and "girl talk" at the home of June Redmond.

year. These provide loving memories each Christmas as they're unpacked. And when the children marry, the boxes will become very special wedding gifts on which the new couple can build their own traditions.

"Rituals and traditions bring families closer together," says June, "and they'll bring your children back home in years to come."

These three believe that Christmas traditions tie families and friendships—the important things of life—together, providing a continuum of past, present, and future. Their philosophy is stated thus:

"Christmas past renews our love of family and friends; Christmas present shines with bright joy and celebration; Christmas future inspires our faith and hopes for all our tomorrows."

Note: The above quotation was taken from *Treasures of the Heart and Hand,* a wonderful little book written by June and Alice and now in its fifth printing. It's packed with "ah-hah" ideas for building your own traditions as well as for country decorating, crafting, cooking, hostessing, and gift giving. For information about how to order a copy, see source listing on page 154.

Below: "Gift wrap is my thing," says June. She always sees that each gift to a special friend is contained in a special wrap. June made these distinctive wraps by painting hearts and holly on plain brown paper or muslin bags. "Anybody can paint holly," June contends.

Handed Down With Love

Winter morning light pours in through lace curtains. The whole morning's ahead, with plenty of time to curl up on Grandmother's quilt and sort through her button jar. By making the projects on these pages, you can pass on such memories, along with bits of your own treasured collection.

Antique Button Brooch

Materials:
1 (1½") covered-button kit
scrap of cream-colored fabric
hot-glue gun and glue sticks
bar-pin accessory
6" (¼"-wide) lace or crocheted edging
thread to match
approximately 24 assorted tiny pearl
  buttons

Remove metal shank from button. Cut fabric and cover button form, following instructions on button-kit package.

Hot-glue bar pin to back of covered button. Gather the lace edging to fit the outer edge of the covered button. Hot-glue edging to button.

Choose a basic design for placement of tiny buttons on covered-button form. (Refer to photograph.) Begin hot-gluing them in place from the center of the covered button out. Glue them in layers for the best coverage.

Crazy-Quilt Fan

Silk from Grandfather's old ties and scraps of velvet, ribbons, and lace can be embellished with crazy-quilting embroidery stitches to make this lavish Victorian-style ornament.

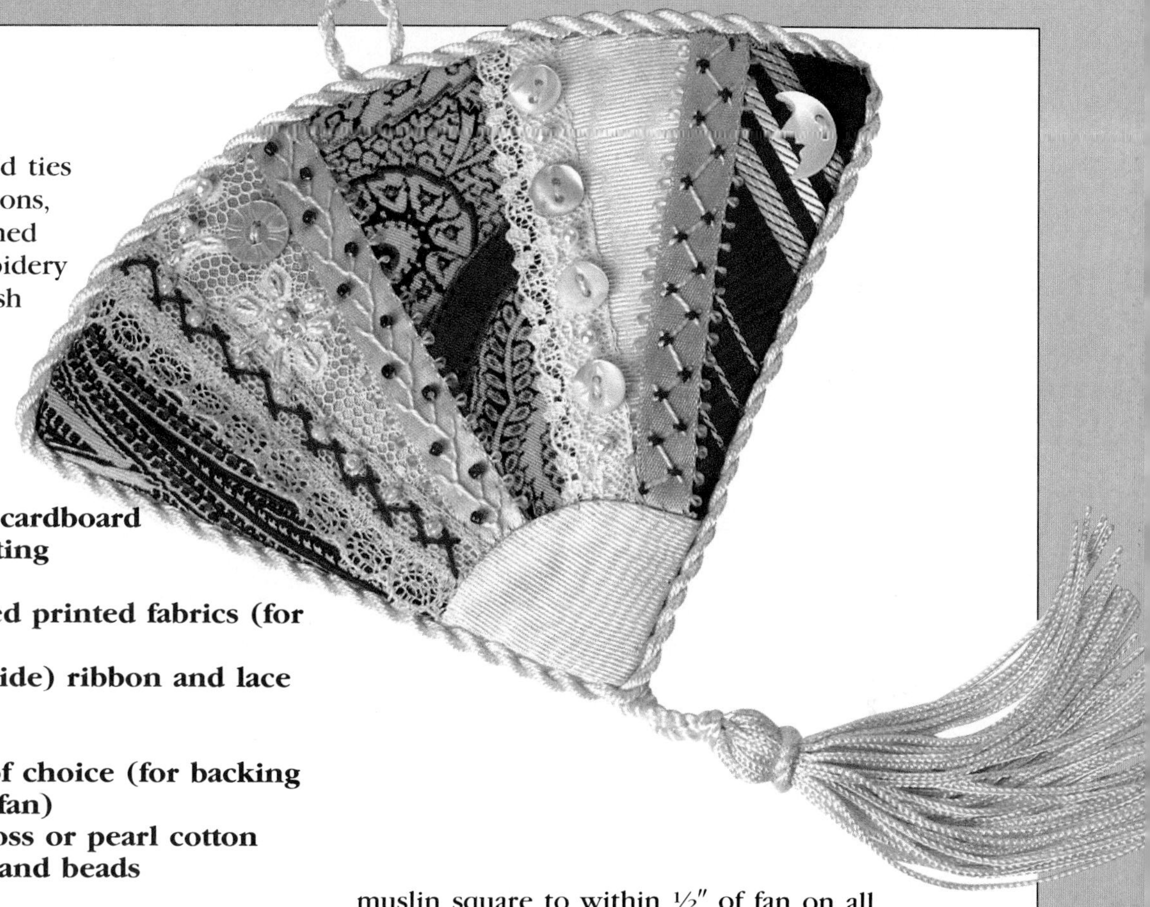

Materials:
tracing paper
2 (6"-square) pieces of cardboard
6" square polyester batting
6" square muslin
2" x 5" scraps of assorted printed fabrics (for fan wedges)
4" lengths (3/8"- to 1/2"-wide) ribbon and lace (for overlays)
thread to match
6" square plain fabric of choice (for backing and bottom piece of fan)
assorted embroidery floss or pearl cotton
assorted small buttons and beads
craft glue
1/2 yard cording
small rayon tassel (to match cording)
thread to match

To make fan pattern, cut a quarter-circle with a 4" radius from tracing paper. Using pattern, cut 2 cardboard fans and one batting fan. Set these aside.

Center and trace pattern on a 6" square of muslin. (Do not cut muslin fan; use lines as placement guides.) Cut 5 (3¾"-long) wedge-shaped pieces from assorted fabrics and cover tracing on muslin with them, overlapping raw edges about ¼". Outer edges should extend ¼" beyond pattern lines. Pin. (See Diagram 1.) Cover overlapped edges with lengths of ribbon or lace and slipstitch through all layers to secure. Turn under ¼" on outer edges of fan and slipstitch to muslin, matching turned-under edge to pattern lines.

Cut a quarter-circle with a 2" radius from backing fabric, turn under ¼" on all sides, and slipstitch to bottom of fan along pattern lines, covering points of wedges. Couch down lengths of ribbon with fancy embroidery stitches. Add beads or buttons for extra embellishment. Trim

muslin square to within ½" of fan on all sides. (See Diagram 2.)

Glue batting fan to one cardboard fan. Center and stretch the embroidered fan over batting. Wrap raw edges of muslin to wrong side of cardboard and glue. Cover second cardboard fan with backing fabric. Place the 2 fans with wrong sides facing, matching edges, and whipstitch along edge to join. Glue or sew cording to cover stitching. Tack tassel to bottom of fan. Tack 3" loop of cording to back for hanger.

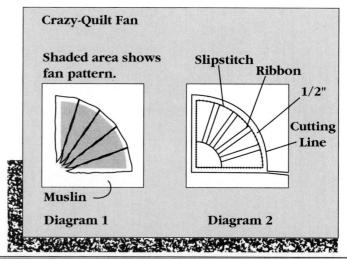

Crazy-Quilt Fan

Shaded area shows fan pattern.

Muslin

Diagram 1

Slipstitch
Ribbon
1/2"
Cutting
Line

Diagram 2

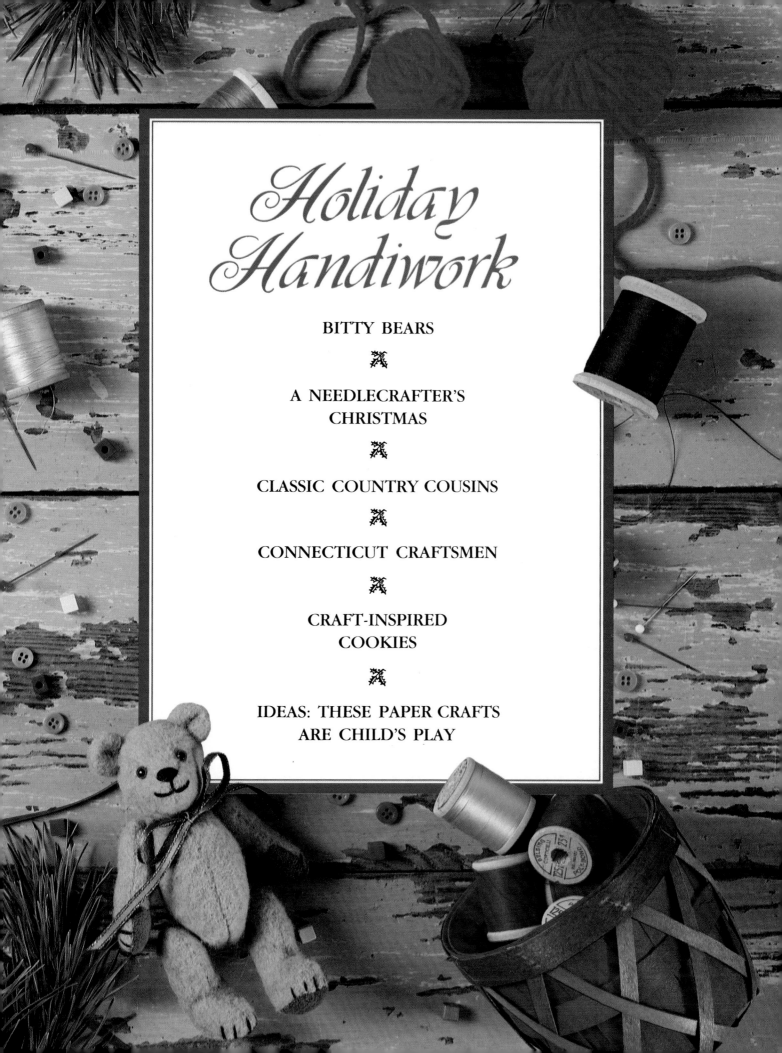

Holiday Handiwork

BITTY BEARS

A NEEDLECRAFTER'S
CHRISTMAS

CLASSIC COUNTRY COUSINS

CONNECTICUT CRAFTSMEN

CRAFT-INSPIRED
COOKIES

IDEAS: THESE PAPER CRAFTS
ARE CHILD'S PLAY

Bitty Bears

Use these miniature critters as tree ornaments or as delightful stocking stuffers.

Materials for one bear:
pattern and diagram on page 145
tracing paper
9″ x 12″ piece of lightweight wool, corduroy, velour, velveteen, or any lightweight fabric with short nap
2″ square of felt or imitation suede
matching sewing thread
polyester stuffing
awl or ice pick
1 set (6mm) plastic eyes with lock washers
black embroidery floss
embroidery needle
small dowel or chopstick for stuffing tool
very fine needle
4 sets (¼″) snaps
⅓ yard (⅛″-wide) ribbon

Transfer pattern to tracing paper. Pin pattern pieces to fabric as indicated and cut out. Transfer pattern markings to fabric. With right sides facing, fold body along center line and, leaving open at neck, stitch together. Clip where indicated and turn. Turn under seam allowance around neck and baste. Stuff body.

With right sides facing, pin and hand-stitch the 2 side head sections from nose to neck front. With right sides facing, pin and baste center head section to side head sections, matching Xs. Using backstitch, hand-stitch from nose to

neck back. Trim seams slightly and turn.

Check positions for eyes by stuffing the head and marking placement with pins. When positions are correct, make holes with awl. Unstuff head and insert eyes, pushing on lock washers as tightly as possible. Restuff head.

Make small tuck in inner ear as indicated. With right sides facing, pin and stitch one inner ear to one outer ear, leaving open on bottom edge. Clip curves and turn. Turn up bottom edge of ear and baste. Trim seams and turn. Repeat for second ear.

Pin ears to sides of head where indicated. Make adjustments, if necessary, and stitch. Using 2 strands of black embroidery floss, embroider nose in satin stitch. Then embroider mouth in backstitch. (See Diagram on page 145.)

With right sides facing, fold arm along center line. Pin and stitch, leaving open between Xs. Clip almost to seam line where indicated. Turn under seam allowance at top of arm between Xs and baste. Trim seam and turn. Repeat for other arm.

Stuff arms firmly, using small dowel or large end of chopstick. Slipstitch tops of arms closed.

With right side of paw pad up, pin pad to inside of paw. Using a very fine needle, overcast paw pad close to all edges. Using 2 strands of black embroidery floss, sew 4 straight lines on top of paw for fingers. (See photograph.) Repeat for other arm.

With right sides facing, fold leg along center line. Pin or baste and stitch, leaving open between Xs and at bottom of foot. Turn under seam allowances at top of leg and baste. Turn up seam allowances on bottom of foot and baste. Trim side seam slightly and turn. Repeat for other leg. With right side out, pin foot pad to bottom of foot. Stitch same as paw pad. With 2 strands of black embroidery floss, sew 4 straight lines on front of foot for toes. (See photograph.) Repeat for other leg. Stuff legs. Slipstitch tops of legs closed.

Slipstitch head to body, matching center neck and center body seams. To prevent head from twisting during sewing, start at center front and stitch around one side to center back of neck. Starting again at center front, stitch around the other side to center back. Sew snaps to arms, legs, and body at dots. Snap arms and legs to body.

Tie a ribbon bow around bear's neck.

A Needlecrafter's Christmas

Here's a potpourri of country Christmas decorating ideas that will showcase your needlework skills and highlight your holiday celebrations. Craft a collection of these sewing box ornaments; combine them with thimbles, scissors, and other tools of the stitcher's trade for a tree that's uniquely yours.

Button Wreath

Materials:
1 yard (1½″-wide) red velvet ribbon
red thread
12″ medium-gauge craft wire
pliers
8″ (1″-wide) red plaid ribbon
12 (⅝″ to ¾″) assorted buttons
10″ (¹⁄₁₆″-wide) red satin ribbon

Turn under ¼″ on both ends of ribbon and finger-press. Stitch down center of ribbon, using a medium-width zigzag. On wrong side of ribbon, gently insert wire between stitches and ribbon, pushing ribbon along wire to gather. Leave ¼″ of wire free on each end. Bend wire gently to form circle. Using pliers, bend ends of wire into small hooks and join, closing hooks to secure. Adjust gathers. Tie a plaid bow and tack to bottom of wreath. Clip bow ends to notch. On front, hand-sew buttons to ribbon along center zigzag seam. Fold satin ribbon in half to form loop and tack to top back to form hanger.

Pincushion Kitty

Materials:
pattern on page 144
2 (4″ x 6″) matching fabric scraps
thread to match
contrasting embroidery floss
polyester stuffing
6 straight pins with plastic heads
6″ (¼″-wide) satin ribbon (to match floss)

Above: A garland made by tying together red skeins and green skeins of embroidery floss with ⅛″ ribbon is nestled among handmade ornaments, sewing notions, and collectibles. Instructions for making the ornaments are simple and fun.

Transfer pattern to wrong side of one piece of fabric. Place fabric pieces with right sides facing and machine-stitch along traced outline to join, leaving open as marked. Trim seam allowance to ¼″, clip curves, and turn. Stuff firmly. Slipstitch opening closed. Transfer embroidery lines to right side of cat.

To start embroidery, insert threaded needle through cat from back and tug thread to pull knot to inside, hiding knot in the stuffing. Using stem stitch and one strand of floss, embroider facial features, ears, legs, and tail. When finished, run needle through to back of cat and take a small backstitch. Then insert needle through to the front, pull hard, and cut off thread close to fabric. (Thread should disappear in cat.) Add straight pins for whiskers. Fold ribbon in half to make loop and tack to back of head.

Heart Pocket

Materials:
pattern on page 144
2 (5" x 8") scraps of cotton fabric
thread to match
medium-weight fusible web
heavy iron-on interfacing
paper or leather punch
12" (¼"-wide) satin ribbon

Stack one piece of fabric (wrong side up), web, interfacing (sticky side up), and second piece of fabric (right side up). Following manufacturer's directions, fuse layers together to create a 2-sided piece of heavy fabric. Transfer pattern to fabric and cut out. Fold fabric along fold line with right sides facing and stitch, using ¼" seam. Clip as indicated, trim seam close to stitching, and turn.

Punch holes in heart as indicated on pattern. Cut ribbon in half. For hangers, insert both loose ends of one ribbon length from inside through holes on one side of basket. Tie loose ends together in a bow on outside of basket. Clip ends. Repeat for other side. Fill with dried flowers or candies, if desired.

Button Man

Materials:
3 (12") lengths fine-gauge florists' wire
4 (½") half-round shank buttons
88 (½") buttons, assorted
12 (¾") buttons, assorted
4 (¼") red wooden beads with holes
1 (¾") white wooden bead with ½" hole
8" (¹⁄₁₆"-wide) red satin ribbon

For arms, cut a length of wire in half, forming 2 (6") pieces. Fold one piece in half. Slip one end of wire through a shank button; slide button down wire to fold. Thread 17 (½") buttons onto wire ends, inserting wire through 2 holes in buttons. Slip both ends of wire through a small bead. (See Diagram 1.) Repeat for other arm. For legs, fold a length of wire in half but do not cut. Follow directions above, beginning with a shank button, then adding 25 (½") buttons and one bead. Repeat for other leg.

For body, slip loose wire ends of left leg through one hole of a ¾" button, and loose wire ends of right leg through opposite hole. (See Diagram 2.) Add ¾" buttons, for a total of 11. Set aside one ¾" button for hat. Add one (½") button on top of body.

For neck, slip loose wire ends of one leg and arm through one hole of one (½") button, and loose wire ends of other leg and arm through other hole. (See Diagram 3.) Add 2 (½") buttons, for a total of 4 neck buttons. Twist all wire ends together just above neck buttons. Leaving 1" above neck, cut off excess wire.

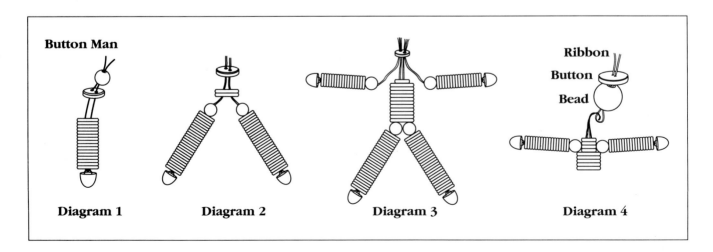

Button Man

Diagram 1   Diagram 2   Diagram 3   Ribbon
                                                          Button
                                                          Bead   Diagram 4

the shell from the outlines. Cut 6 felt shapes. Stack felt shapes on top of each other and whip-stitch edges together.

Fold velvet strip in half lengthwise. Insert curved edge of felt shape in fold of velvet strip, covering felt edges. (See Diagram.) With floss, attach raw edges of velvet to felt shape with running stitches taken back and forth through the stacked felt. Cut excess velvet from sides. (Raw edges will be covered by shell.)

Place felt inside shell halves. Sew through hole at shell bottom to close. Thread ribbon through hole at top and knot close to shell. Knot loose ends of ribbon, forming hanger. Insert pins in velvet strip. (See photograph.)

To attach head, turn wire ends under ¼" to form a small hook. Thread the last ¾" button to the center of ribbon. Leaving a long loop at the bottom, thread the other half of the ribbon through the other hole. Insert the loop through large bead and then slip loop over wire hook. (See Diagram 4.) Slide hook through bead. Tie knot in ribbon at top of button to secure. Knot loose ends of ribbon to form hanger.

Shell Pincushion

Materials:
2 medium or large matched scallop shells
sharp craft knife
felt scraps
scissors
1"-wide bias strip of velvet or velveteen (to fit around shell plus ½")
thread to match
embroidery floss to match velvet
needle
6" (¹⁄₁₆"-wide) satin ribbon to match velvet
small straight pins with plastic heads

Gently twirl point of craft knife into shell to form small holes at top and bottom of each half. Trace 6 outlines of shell onto felt, eliminating the small projections or "wings" at the base of

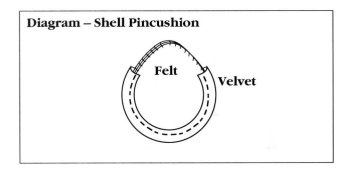

Diagram – Shell Pincushion

Felt   Velvet

Cross-Stitched Ohio Star

Materials:
chart and color key on page 144
4" square perforated paper
embroidery floss (see color key)
pinking shears
craft knife
6" (¼"-wide) satin ribbon

Using 3 strands of floss, center and stitch design on perforated paper, following chart for design. With pinking shears, trim paper on all sides, at least 3 holes from the stitching.

Referring to chart, use craft knife to cut away the paper within the small rectangle of back-stitching for the ribbon hanger. Thread ribbon through this hole and knot ends together.

Ohio Star Stocking and Tree Skirt

Materials for stocking:
pattern and diagram on pages 142–143
cardboard or plastic template material
⅓ yard (45″-wide) red pindot (fabric A)
⅓ yard (45″-wide) white miniprint
  (fabric B)
8″ x 10″ piece green miniprint (fabric C)
⅓ yard (45″-wide) red miniprint (fabric D)
12″ x 15″ piece of muslin
⅓ yard of batting
chalk or fabric pencil
white quilting thread

Note: All seam allowances are ¼″. Seams should be pressed toward darker fabric when possible. Never press seams open.

Extend whole stocking pattern as directed. Transfer all pattern pieces to template material and cut out. Cut pieces from fabric as indicated.

Following Diagram 1, join pieces as indicated

Above: Trim your mantel with a quilted Ohio Star stocking and lots of easy-to-make heart pockets.

to form stocking front. Press all seams.

Place stocking back (fabric A) and pieced stocking front right sides facing, keeping upper edges even. Trim excess material at lower edge of stocking front even with back. Turning under edges of appliqué hearts ¼″, appliqué onto toe as shown in Diagram 1. Transfer small heart pattern, without seam allowance, to template material. Using chalk or fabric pencil, trace hearts onto each fabric A square as indicated.

Place one batting stocking between the muslin stocking and the pieced stocking front. Baste ¼″ from outer edge through all layers. Outline-quilt hearts with white quilting thread through all layers.

Baste remaining batting stocking to wrong side of stocking back. With right sides facing, stitch stocking front to stocking back, leaving top edge open. Turn.

Cut a 24″ x 2½″ strip from fabric B for ruffle. Fold lengthwise with wrong sides facing; press. Tuck ends under ¼″ and press. Gather ¼″ from long raw edges. With right sides facing and raw edges even, stitch ruffle to top of stocking.

To construct the hanger, cut a 5″ x 2″ strip from fabric B. With right sides facing, fold the strip in half lengthwise and stitch long edge. Turn. Fold in half, forming loop, and stitch to the corner of the stocking.

With right sides of fabric D lining pieces facing, stitch lining, leaving top and 3″ along toe open for turning. With right sides facing, place stocking inside lining.

Aligning the top edges, sew through all layers around the top of stocking. Turn stocking through opening in toe. Stitch opening closed. Slide lining inside stocking.

Materials for tree skirt:
pattern and diagram on page 143
cardboard or plastic template material
1½ yards (45″-wide) red pindot (fabric A)
⅓ yard (45″-wide) white miniprint
  (fabric B)
⅓ yard (45″-wide) green miniprint
  (fabric C)
½ yard fabric C for ruffle
⅛ yard (45″-wide) red miniprint (fabric D)
1⅓ yards fabric D for backing
1⅓ yards of batting
white quilting thread
chalk or fabric pencil

Above: This tree skirt features the traditional Ohio Star quilt block pattern. Stitched in red and green calico and embellished with quilted hearts, it brings an old-fashioned touch to your Needlecrafter's Christmas.

Note: All seam allowances are ¼". Seams should be pressed toward darker fabric when possible. Never press seams open.

Transfer pattern pieces to cardboard and cut out. Cut pieces from fabric as indicated. Cut 5 (6½" x 6¼") rectangles from fabric B.

Following the shaded area of Diagram 1, construct 8 Ohio Star blocks. Press seams. Form a strip by joining one star block, one plain rectangle, and one star block. (See Diagram 2.) Repeat for 3 more strips. Press. (Set aside the remaining plain rectangle for center.)

Fold 1⅛ yards of fabric A in half twice to form quarters. Working from folded corner, draw a quarter-circle arc with a 19¼" radius. (See Diagram 3.) Pin layers together and cut along arc. Next cut along fold lines to form 4 wedges. With right sides facing, sew a strip to right edge of each wedge. Join center rectangle to end of one of the strips, and continue to sew strip-wedge sections together to form circle. Leave last section unjoined to form opening to

fit around tree. Press seams. Referring to Diagram 2 for placement, trace large heart quilting pattern on fabric, using chalk or fabric pencil.

On wrong side, trace 4" circle in center of center rectangle. Draw straight line from open wedge section to closest point on traced circle.

For ruffle, cut 5 (3½" x 45") strips of fabric C. Join strips at selvage edges to form one long strip. With wrong sides facing, fold strip lengthwise with raw edges even. Press. Gather ruffle along raw edge. With raw edges even, baste ruffle to outside edge of skirt.

From bottom to top, layer batting, backing fabric (right side up), and tree skirt top (wrong side up). (Backing fabric and top should have right sides facing.) Pin outside edges, along straight line, and around circle in center rectangle, securing all layers. Trim batting and backing even with circumference of skirt.

Leaving a 6" opening for turning along one straight edge, sew all edges through all layers. Cut opening in backing and batting to match opening in top, trimming center circle to ¼" from stitching line. Turn. Lightly press. Hand-stitch opening closed. Quilt large heart outlines through all layers of fabric.

Classic Country Cousins

Pigtails, straw hats, and rosy cheeks make these dolls unmistakably country.

Materials for one doll:
pattern on pages 148–149
tracing paper
⅓ yard (36″-wide) muslin for doll
⅓ yard (36″-wide) fabric A for dress
¼ yard (36″-wide) fabric B for overskirt
1 small scrap of fabric C for apple pocket
1 small scrap of fabric D for stem
¼ yard (36″-wide) fabric E for bloomers
matching thread
stuffing
brown, peach embroidery flosses
blusher
cotton swab
1 package of Feel O' Fleece
⅔ yard (⅛″-wide) elastic
purchased straw hat to fit

Note: All seams are ¼″ unless otherwise indicated.

Transfer pattern to tracing paper. Pin pattern to fabric and cut out pieces as directed. Transfer all pattern markings to fabric.

With right sides facing, pin doll back and front together. Stitch, leaving open where indicated. Clip curves and turn.

Stuff arms and legs firmly to within 1″ of tops. To allow arms and legs to bend, sew seams through both layers of fabric across upper arms and upper legs as indicated on pattern. Stuff body and head. Whipstitch opening closed.

Using one strand of brown floss, embroider eyes in satin stitch. With one strand of peach floss, embroider nose and mouth in outline stitch; then embroider cheek circles in running stitch. With cotton swab, apply blush inside stitched cheeks.

To make wig, cut a piece of the Feel O' Fleece, 15″ x 4″. Hand-stitch crosswise down center. With small backstitches, sew center of wig to center of head. For bangs, cut a piece of Feel O' Fleece, 3″ x 1″. Draw fleece together in center with one stitch. Sew center of bangs to center front of head at X. To make pigtails, secure fleece to sides of head at Xs with several large stitches through head and over fleece. Divide fleece into 3 equal sections and braid. Tie ends of braids with thread.

To make dress, cut back piece down center. With right sides facing, sew back seam from bottom to dot. Press seam open. Hem each side of back opening. With right sides facing, sew front to back at shoulder seams and press seams open. Sew underarm and side seams and press seams open. Sew a ⅜″ hem around bottom of dress.

Press neck opening under ¼″ and sew a gathering stitch all around but do not fasten off. Repeat for sleeve openings. Place dress on doll and gather neck and sleeve openings to fit. Tie off. Blindstitch back opening closed.

To make overskirt, cut an 8″ x 22″ rectangle from fabric B. With right sides facing, fold piece in half crosswise and sew ends together with a ¼″ seam. Press seam open. Sew a ⅜″ hem around bottom of skirt. Turn under ¼″ at waist and press. Turn under ¼″ again at waist to form casing. Press. Sew close to bottom edge of casing, leaving a small opening. Cut piece of elastic 5½″ long. Thread elastic through casing and sew ends together. Sew opening closed.

With right sides facing, sew apple pieces together, leaving opening as indicated. Clip curves, turn, and press. For apple stem, cut a 2⅜″ x 1½″ rectangle. Fold both long sides of rectangle to inside with raw edges meeting at center back. Press. Fold in half lengthwise again down center, having raw edges on inside of fold. Press. Fold this strip in half crosswise to form a loop. Place ends of loop in opening in apple and blindstitch opening closed. Referring to photograph for placement, blindstitch apple to skirt, leaving open at the top. Place overskirt over dress.

To make bloomers, place pieces right sides facing and sew center seam. Clip curve. Sew inside leg seams. Turn under ¼″ at waist and press. Turn under ¼″ again at waist to form casing. Press. Sew close to bottom edge of casing, leaving a small opening. Repeat for bottom of each leg. Cut 4½″ of elastic for each leg and a 5½″ length for waist. Thread elastic through casings and sew ends together. Sew casings closed. Place bloomers on doll. Place hat on doll's head.

Connecticut Craftsmen

They built their handsome home themselves, and it is alight with wit and whimsy—playful words and imagery are carved, etched, and inlaid into its very fabric.

If you believe that the personal touch of handiwork adds special meaning to a home at any time of the year and is an essential part of the holiday season, then artists Tommy Simpson and Missy Stevens are sure to inspire you. They built their handsome home themselves, and it is alight with wit and whimsy—playful words and imagery are carved, etched, and inlaid into its very fabric. Their Christmas decorations are infused with the same good humor.

Tommy and Missy's house, nestled in the wooded Connecticut countryside, features two very important rooms. Their studios are wondrous spaces filled with all the creative trappings you would expect of Santa's workshop. Missy works her loom in an upstairs studio, making woven pictures and rugs animated with images from nature. In her weaving, she uses long strips torn from secondhand corduroy pants, which provide a rich palette of soft hues. Tommy's studio is in a wing of the house. At any given time, he may have a painting, a one-of-a-kind piece of furniture, and a sculpture under way. Though Tommy and Missy work in different mediums, it's clear that this is a marriage of mutual admiration and inspiration.

Tommy and Missy have a knack for turning just about anything into art, and many of their holiday decorations are made from everyday scrap materials. And they have amassed a fascinating collection of ornaments, always keeping an eye out for their favorite kinds.

According to Missy, "It's especially fun to look for ornaments when we travel. One year we were in Mexico at Christmastime. We found painted tin ornaments, as well as carved gourds, which lent themselves as ornaments." On their tree, every crook of a branch is embellished.

Above: Every ornament has a story behind it. Missy marvels at the power of Christmas memories: "It's amazing how, when we get out the ornaments every year, we can recall details about every one of them—who made them, where and when we found them, what inspired them."

Antique and reproduction German glass balls, glass birds, beaded baubles, Santa-shaped ornaments, chenille-and-paper assemblages, and tinsel trimmings mingle with ornaments created by Tommy and Missy and their artist friends.

The photographs of Tommy and Missy's home, here and on the next few pages, reveal their great love and appreciation of tradition. Although obviously influenced by the past, Tommy and Missy bring their own creativity and personal fancies to every detail of their surroundings, including their Christmas decorations. This combination makes for a charming homeplace, an almost magical place in the heart of the holiday season.

Left: Over the garlanded Dutch door, "Howdy" is carved in capital letters. That happy greeting and the appealing word "Butterplum" epitomize the welcoming wit of this house.

Left: Standing guard over the snow-mounded garden is a scarecrow, imparting more mirth than menace. Made of junk, he has a wooden box body, a snow-shovel head with funnel eyes, and rubber-glove hands. Years ago, when Tommy and Missy were preparing for a move, junk accumulated, and Tommy was drawn to the pile. He and Missy shaped 10 scarecrows from the castoffs. Their recycling efforts brought a tidy sum—they sold the sculptures to neighbors and passersby for $100 apiece.

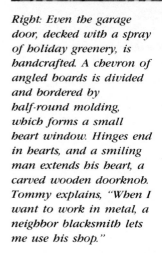

Right: Even the garage door, decked with a spray of holiday greenery, is handcrafted. A chevron of angled boards is divided and bordered by half-round molding, which forms a small heart window. Hinges end in hearts, and a smiling man extends his heart, a carved wooden doorknob. Tommy explains, "When I want to work in metal, a neighbor blacksmith lets me use his shop."

Above: Watch where you're going! This playful gingerbread man with dapper dowel "buttons" is inset into the lovely and durable maple floor. For Tommy, every surface is an artistic opportunity. Other floor motifs include butterflies, flowers, and birds. When children come to visit, they're sent in search of particular shapes. There's mischief afoot here—some images are hiding under rugs!

Below: In a Christmas history book, Tommy read how someone preserved a tree to use the following year. After the needles dropped, every branch of the big tree was wrapped in cotton. To Tommy, the idea of someone carefully wrapping every branch was wonderful and funny at the same time. He decided to make his own. His tree—built with dowels and wire, wrapped in batting, and decorated with beaded baubles—is smaller and less intricate than the real thing, but it captures the charm of its inspiration.

The chair is a collaboration between Tommy and his mother. He made the frame and designed the needlepoint cover. His mother did the stitchery. (A smaller ladies' chair is in the works.) The shelf of miniature chairs—doll furniture and samples—helps Tommy communicate with clients for commissions.

The framed mittens are Tommy's prize. He won the services of a knitting artist in a fund-raising auction and requested these amusing mittens. The one on the left with a red thumb and cotton beard is "santa thumarius."

Right: This German feather tree, trimmed with the couple's German glass ornaments, was purchased. However, Tommy created the miniature scene beneath the tree, his version of a traditional Moravian decoration called a putz. He sponge-painted the fence with "snow." The table and chairs, made from English oak, cherry, and ash, are also his work. The chairs have hearts, words, and shapes suggestive of growing things. The wall hanging is an antique hooked rug, a gift to Missy from Tommy. Teapots, also favorite collectibles, line a high shelf.

Above: The mantel beam, inscribed "Meadowdale Farm," is from Tommy's grandfather's farm in Illinois. The dramatically grained wooden panel is from a mahogany tree crotch, the area where the main trunk forks into branches. The small drawer holds matches. Missy decorated the mantel with a garland of greenery, dried flowers, and ornaments.

Tommy and Missy possess the captivating presence of folks who revel in their work. Tommy says simply, "Life's too short. You should love what you do."

Above: Tommy surprised Missy one Christmas with this Noah's ark. That first year, he carved several pairs of animals but painted only one set. Each year they paint a few sets, and Tommy carves some new ones. Missy contributed locks of her hair for animals' tails.

Tommy and Missy's Scrap Craft Ornaments

Missy made the ornaments pictured at right. The reddish hearts are felted double-weave cutouts, the beige heart is a piece of a quilt, and the pom-poms are made with yarn.

To make your own pom-poms, wrap yarn around and around three fingers or a piece of cardboard. Slip the bundle off and tie it in the middle with yarn. Leave extra yarn on this tie. (If a bundle doesn't seem full enough, make another one and tie them together at the center.)

Experiment with yarn, string, paper strips, metallic trims, ribbons, and even feathers. Missy says, "You can achieve different patterns, depending on how you introduce the materials into the wrapping."

The next step is to cut the loops on the bundle. Then to loosen the yarn's twist, soak the bundle in warm water for a few minutes. Squeeze out excess water, and slap the bundle against the sink. As the bundle dries, trim it into a round shape and fluff it out. (Some kinds of yarn fluff up more than others.) For a hanger, tie a ribbon to the center tie; then trim the tie.

The colorful critters pictured above were inspired when Missy took trash to the dump and spotted discarded wallpaper samples. According to Tommy, "Missy came back with more than she left with." To make use of this find, they invited friends to an ornament-making party.

To make paper-scrap ornaments of your own, gather poster board, colorful papers and trims, and craft glue. Ask a wallpaper store for discontinued paper books, or use gift wrap paper or magazine pages for backgrounds. Look for novelty trims in fabric, craft, paper, and art supply stores.

Sketch favorite shapes for patterns. (Children's books or cookie cutters are great design sources.) For each ornament, cut one shape from poster board and two from different patterned papers. Cover each side of the board with paper. Add trims. For a hanger, sandwich in a length of floss.

Put a Little Punch in Your Christmas

Punch embroidery adds an extra dimension—texture—to the vibrant colors of ordinary embroidery. Using a special tool called a punch needle and your choice of yarn, a variety of textures can be accomplished—from a thick nubby pile to a soft delicate plush.

Use this interesting craft to create our three country cats. They make sensational ornaments for your own tree, or you can wrap them up as gifts for your cat-loving friends.

Your local craft dealer can supply you with the needed tools and materials for this project. Punch needles are available in three sizes, allowing for the use of different sizes and numbers of strands of yarn. The needles come with needle-threader and instructions. With the punch needle, you work from the underside of your project, punching down to form loops on the top. (See Diagram on following page.) The technique is simple. Once you've mastered it, the work goes very quickly. Instructions are on the following page.

Materials for three cats:
patterns on page 146
3 (12″) squares of tightly woven fabric
8″ screw-type embroidery hoop
size 3 punch-needle kit with threader,
  guards, and instructions
2-ply acrylic yarn in colors indicated on
  patterns
mylar or cardboard template material
3 (8″ x 5″) pieces posterboard or lightweight
  cardboard
3 (8″ x 5″) pieces of felt to match cats
1 yard (⅛″-wide) red ribbon
red thread
3 (¾″) gold bells
white glue

Transfer one of the country-cat patterns to the wrong side of each 12″ square of tightly woven fabric. (Medium-weight interfacing material works well.) Place the fabric in screw-type embroidery hoop with the traced design up. (Punch embroidery is worked from the wrong side of the fabric.) Place the B guard on the punch needle.

Following the manufacturer's instructions, which come with the punch-needle kit, work each cat in the colors indicated on the patterns or in colors of your choice. Work all outlining first. Next, work all of the small areas, such as eyes, nose, mouth, etc. Finally, fill in all remaining large areas.

Remove the finished piece from the hoop. Trim the fabric to ¼″ around the embroidered cat. Turn under the raw edge of the fabric to the edge of the embroidery and baste fabric to the back of the cat.

Transfer each of the country-cat patterns to the template material. Cut one posterboard cat piece and one felt cat piece to fit each of the finished punched cats. Glue the posterboard cat pieces to the backs of the punched cats. Glue each of the felt cat pieces to the backs of the posterboard pieces.

Cut a 6″ length of ⅛″-wide red ribbon for each finished cat. Tie bows. With matching thread, tack gold bells to the middle back of each bow. Tack or glue the bows in place on the cats.

Cut another 6″ length of ⅛″-wide red ribbon. Form a loop with the ribbon and glue it to the back of the cat for hanging.

Diagram – Punch Embroidery Technique

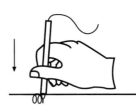

1. Punch all the way down.

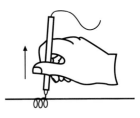

2. Raise needle just to surface.

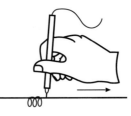

3. Drag needle tip, keeping needle eye facing stitches.

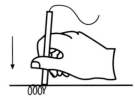

4. Punch all the way down.

A History of Punch Embroidery

Punch embroidery is a very old craft. It's a form of rug hooking that is usually thought of as American folk art but that actually dates back to fifth-century Egypt. It has also been traced to the Vikings, who used it to make thick wraps to protect themselves in Scandinavian winters.

The craft was brought to the American colonies from Europe. And although it soon became a distinctly American art, the art was born of necessity. Early pioneers used strips of wool fabric cut from old clothing to make warm, sturdy bed and floor coverings. Rug hooks and punch needles were fashioned from nails or old forks. Designs were drawn onto feed sacks, which served as foundation material, before burlap became widely available by the yard.

The primitive designs of early 19th-century American rugs are enjoying renewed popularity today. And when scaled down for the art of punch embroidery, the technique can be used for smaller projects to add warmth to your holiday.

Craft-Inspired Cookies

The scent of freshly baked goodies brings back a pleasant childhood memory: Mom has just pulled a batch of warm spicy cookies from the oven; Grandmother is knitting some last stitches on a tiny pair of red mittens; a quiet song floats in over the radio. It would be just another peaceful winter afternoon except for one thing—the cookies are for Christmas.

Now is your chance to make some pleasant seasonal memories for your own family. To help, we offer six great holiday recipes for cookies, inspired by six traditional country crafts. The texture of woven baskets, the rich color combinations of redware pottery, and the fine stitching of quilts are evident in the cookies that fill the following pages. You'll also find the iridescence of stained-glass windows, the delicacy of lace, and the quiet simplicity of a stencil design.

Above: A pastry bag helps you weave these edible baskets quickly and artistically. The satisfying combination of chocolate and peanut butter assures you that these cookies will disappear quickly, too.

Chocolate-Peanut Butter Basket-Weave Cookies

1 (1-ounce) square unsweetened chocolate
½ cup butter or margarine, softened
½ cup creamy peanut butter
¾ cup firmly packed dark brown sugar
2 eggs
1 teaspoon vanilla extract
1¾ cups all-purpose flour
½ teaspoon baking powder
¼ teaspoon salt

Place chocolate in top of a double boiler. Place over simmering water and cook, stirring frequently, until chocolate melts. Remove from heat and cool slightly.

Cream butter and peanut butter in a medium bowl; add brown sugar, beating at medium speed of an electric mixer until light and fluffy. Add eggs and vanilla, beating well. Combine flour, baking powder, and salt; gradually add to creamed mixture, mixing well. Divide dough in half and stir melted chocolate into 1 portion.

Working with one-sixth of each portion of dough at a time, spoon chocolate dough into a pastry bag fitted with a No. 12 round tip. Spoon peanut butter dough into a second pastry bag fitted with a ½-inch-wide No. 48 basket-weave tip. Pipe cookies into a 3-inch-square basket-weave design onto ungreased cookie sheets, alternating chocolate and peanut butter dough.

To achieve basket-weave design, pipe a 3-inch vertical line, using round tip. Using basket-weave tip, pipe short horizontal strips at ½-inch intervals across vertical line. Use round tip to pipe a second 3-inch vertical line down side of basket work, parallel to first vertical line and just covering ends of basket work. Use basket-weave tip to pipe short horizontal strips from first vertical line across second vertical line, filling gaps between first basket-weave strip. Continue piping procedure to achieve a 3-inch square, trimming edges of cookies with a sharp knife, if necessary. Replenish pastry bags with dough as needed. (See front cookie. For rear cookie pictured, reverse tips and follow above procedure.)

Bake cookies at 350° for 10 to 12 minutes. Cool 1 minute on cookie sheets; transfer to wire racks to cool completely. Store cookies in an airtight container. Yield: 1½ dozen.

Above: The skillfully crafted redware plates created by potter Ned Foltz of Reinholds, Pennsylvania, were the inspiration for these pumpkin and whole wheat cookies. Add your own artistic touch with a light creamy icing. Recipe is on page 100.

Opposite: Even if you've never gotten around to finishing your favorite quilt, you can still make batch after batch of these spicy quilted cookie squares. A thimble can play cookie-cutter-for-a-day to use up the leftover odd shapes. Recipe is on pages 100–101.

Redware Pumpkin Cookies

¾ cup butter or margarine, softened
1¾ cups firmly packed brown sugar
¾ cup cooked, mashed pumpkin
2 eggs, beaten
1 tablespoon grated orange rind
3 tablespoons orange juice
2¾ cups all-purpose flour
1¾ cups whole wheat flour
2 teaspoons pumpkin pie spice
½ teaspoon salt
¼ teaspoon baking soda
Orange paste food coloring
Icing (recipe follows)

Cream butter; add sugar, beating well at medium speed of an electric mixer. Add next 4 ingredients; beat until well blended. Combine flours, spice, salt, and soda; gradually stir into creamed mixture. Add food coloring to reach desired tint, mixing well after each addition. Cover and chill for several hours or overnight.

Roll dough to ¼-inch thickness on a wax paper-lined surface; cut dough with a 4½-inch round cookie cutter. Carefully remove cookies from wax paper and place 1 inch apart on lightly greased cookie sheets. Bake at 375° for 8 to 10 minutes. Remove from cookie sheets and cool completely on wire racks.

Spoon icing into a pastry bag fitted with a No. 4 round tip. Pipe icing on cookies to resemble designs on redware pottery. Store cookies in an airtight container between sheets of wax paper. Yield: about 2 dozen.

Icing:

¼ cup shortening
2¼ cups sifted powdered sugar
3 tablespoons half-and-half
¼ teaspoon vanilla extract
2 tablespoons cocoa
Lemon-yellow paste food coloring
Orange paste food coloring

Cream shortening; add sugar alternately with half-and-half and vanilla. Beat with an electric mixer to reach desired consistency.

Divide icing in half; add cocoa to 1 portion and beat well. Add colorings to remaining portion, mixing until icing is golden. Yield: 1 cup.

Quilted Spice Cookies

¼ cup butter or margarine, softened
½ cup firmly packed brown sugar
½ cup dark molasses
3½ cups all-purpose flour
1 teaspoon baking soda
1 teaspoon ground ginger
¾ teaspoon ground cinnamon
½ teaspoon salt
½ teaspoon ground cloves
¼ teaspoon ground nutmeg
¼ cup milk

Select a simple patchwork design and draw it on a 3½-inch square piece of graph paper, using the graph paper lines to help true the design. Make lines of evenly spaced dots along the lines of the design. Set pattern aside.

Cream butter in a large bowl; add brown sugar, beating well at medium speed of a heavy-duty electric mixer. Add molasses, beating until well blended. Sift together flour and next 6 ingredients. Sift again and add to creamed mixture alternately with milk, beginning and ending with flour mixture. Beat well after each addition. Divide dough in half and wrap each portion in wax paper; chill at least 1 hour.

Working with 1 portion of dough at a time, roll dough to ¼-inch thickness on a lightly greased cookie sheet. Freeze dough on cookie sheet 15 minutes or until firm. For first cookie, use a pushpin to prick the patchwork design through the paper pattern onto the dough. Cut out cookie with a sharp knife or pastry wheel, using edges of paper pattern as a guide. Carefully remove paper pattern from first cookie, leaving rolled dough intact on cookie sheet.

To make additional cookies, place pricked paper pattern on dough, rough side down, allowing 1 to 2 inches between edges of cookies. Gently rub over lines of design with your finger to transfer a faint impression to surface of cookie. Cut out cookie with a sharp knife or pastry wheel, using edges of paper pattern as a guide. Remove paper pattern and repeat procedure with remaining dough on cookie sheet.

Carefully remove the excess dough around the cookies and combine it with the remaining dough in the refrigerator. Prick a design into each cookie, using a pushpin. Repeat the entire procedure with the remaining portion of chilled dough. Reserve the remaining dough scraps to make the Thimble Cookie Variation, if desired.

Bake cookies at 350° for 8 minutes or until crisp. Remove from cookie sheets and cool on wire racks. Store cookies in an airtight container. Yield: about 1½ dozen.

Thimble Cookie Variation:

Roll Quilted Cookie dough scraps to ¼-inch thickness on a lightly floured surface. Sprinkle dough lightly with ground cinnamon and sugar and cut with a floured thimble. Transfer cookies to a lightly greased cookie sheet. Bake at 350° for 4 to 5 minutes or until crisp. Remove from cookie sheet and cool. Yield: about 6 dozen.

Stained-Glass Candy Cookies

Peppermint or assorted-flavor hard candies
½ cup butter or margarine, softened
½ cup sugar
1¾ cups all-purpose flour
½ cup finely crushed graham cracker crumbs
¼ teaspoon baking powder
2 tablespoons buttermilk
¾ teaspoon each vanilla, butter, and nut flavorings

Crush each flavor of hard candy separately, using a mortar and pestle. Set aside.

Cream butter in a large bowl; gradually add sugar, beating well at medium speed of an electric mixer.

Combine flour, graham cracker crumbs, and baking powder; add to creamed mixture alternately with buttermilk, beginning and ending with flour mixture. Beat well after each addition. Stir in flavoring.

Roll dough to ¼-inch thickness on a lightly floured surface, using a rolling pin fitted with a pastry sock. Cut dough with 3½-inch assorted holiday-shaped cookie cutters. Cut centers from cookies with smaller assorted cutters. Carefully transfer cookies to aluminum foil-lined cookie sheets. Fill centers with crushed candies to resemble stained glass. If desired, make a small hole in top of each cookie for ribbon hanger.

Bake cookies at 350° for 6 to 8 minutes or just until cookies are done and candy has melted (overbaking will produce dull, unattractive colors). Cool completely on cookie sheets; carefully remove from foil. Store cookies in an airtight container between sheets of wax paper. Yield: about 2 dozen.

Below: These Stained-Glass Candy Cookies will catch your eye as well as the light. Use them as ornaments in a sunny spot, but don't expect them to hang anywhere for long—they're too tempting.

Toasted Oatmeal Lace Cookies

1 cup quick-cooking, pan-toasted oats, uncooked
1 cup sugar
2 tablespoons plus 1 teaspoon all-purpose flour
⅛ teaspoon salt
⅛ teaspoon ground cinnamon
Dash of ground nutmeg
½ cup butter or margarine, melted
1 egg, beaten
1 teaspoon almond extract
1 teaspoon vanilla extract

Combine oats and next 5 ingredients in a medium bowl, stirring well. Add butter, egg, and flavorings; stir until well combined.

Drop oat mixture by teaspoonfuls 3 inches apart onto aluminum foil-lined cookie sheets. Bake at 350° for 6 to 8 minutes or until edges are lightly browned. Cool completely before carefully removing from foil. Store cookies in an airtight container between sheets of wax paper. Yield: about 6 dozen.

Below: Toasted oatmeal blends with spices and almond flavoring to give these Lace Cookies a distinctive taste and a delicate crunch.

Christmas Cottage Stenciled Cookies

½ cup butter or margarine, softened
½ cup sugar
½ cup firmly packed brown sugar
2¾ cups all-purpose flour
¼ cup cocoa
½ teaspoon baking soda
¼ teaspoon ground cinnamon
½ cup commercial eggnog
1 egg white, lightly beaten
Sifted powdered sugar
Red round and heart-shaped cinnamon candies

Duplicate and cut out the Christmas Cottage pattern found on page 138. Design and cut stencils for roof, chimney, door, and windows in proportion to the Christmas Cottage pattern, using paper doilies. Set the pattern and stencils aside.

Cream butter in a large bowl; add sugars, beating well at medium speed of an electric mixer. Combine flour, cocoa, soda, and cinnamon; add to creamed mixture alternately with eggnog, beginning and ending with flour mixture. Beat well after each addition. Divide dough in half and wrap each portion in wax paper; chill at least 2 hours.

Working with 1 portion of dough at a time, roll dough to ¼-inch thickness on a wax paper-lined surface. Freeze dough on wax paper 15 minutes or until firm. Cut each cookie from dough with a sharp knife, using edges of the Christmas Cottage pattern as a guide. Carefully remove cookies from wax paper and place 1 inch apart on lightly greased cookie sheets. Repeat procedure with remaining portion of chilled dough. Bake at 375° for 6 to 8 minutes. Cool 1 minute on cookie sheets; transfer to wire racks to cool completely.

Lightly brush cookies with egg white; allow to dry slightly. Place stencils on each cookie, arranging in a pattern to resemble features found on a house (roof, chimney, door, and windows); sprinkle with powdered sugar. Carefully remove stencils and repeat procedure with remaining cookies. Decorate with cinnamon candies, using remaining egg white to attach. Store cookies in an airtight container between sheets of wax paper. Yield: ½ dozen.

A Christmas Cottage To Stitch

Materials for ornament and pot holder:
pattern on page 138
tissue paper
¼ yard brown pindot fabric
¼ yard white miniprint fabric
¼ yard lightweight iron-on interfacing
¼ yard polyester batting
scraps of red miniprint, green miniprint,
  and solid yellow fabric
9″ (⅜″-wide) decorative Christmas ribbon
9″ (⅜″-wide) white lace
scrap of fusible web
2 (⅝″) red shank heart buttons
1 tiny white star button
hot-glue gun and glue sticks
13½″ (⅛″-wide) red minidot ribbon for
  ornament
13½″ (⅜″-wide) red minidot ribbon for pot
  holder
matching thread
1 ounce cinnamon spice potpourri

Left: You can stitch and *bake this Christmas Cottage. The cookie cottage is lightly dusted with "snow" on the outside. Inside, there's a hint of eggnog.*

Note: Instructions for ornament and pot holder are the same.

Transfer pattern to tissue paper. (For ornament, reduce pattern 50% and then transfer to tissue paper.) Back all fabrics to be used for appliqué with lightweight iron-on interfacing. Cut out pieces as indicated on pattern.

Arrange appliqués on cottage with Christmas ribbon and lace running horizontally from bottom of left roof corner to bottom of right roof corner. Cut small pieces of fusible web and fuse appliqués, ribbon, and lace in place on cottage.

Appliqué roof, windows, door, and door window, using medium-width satin stitch. Topstitch outside edges of Christmas ribbon and lace to cottage, using matching thread. Using contrasting thread, topstitch window panes and door window detail as indicated on pattern. Appliqué snow to top of chimney, using medium-width satin stitch. Set aside.

Cut rectangles of red miniprint fabric (backing) and batting slightly larger than cottage piece. With batting on bottom, red fabric right side up, and cottage piece right side down, pin all pieces together. Stitch around cottage, using ¼″ seam. Leave opening at bottom and opening for chimney as indicated on pattern. Trim batting and backing even with cottage.

To create a spicy aroma, insert a small amount of cinnamon potpourri between batting and red miniprint fabric.

Pin chimney front and back together, with right sides facing. Stitch sides and top, using ⅛″ seam. Clip corners, turn right side out, lightly stuff with small snips of batting, and trim chimney at an angle to fit into opening on roof. Insert chimney and hand-stitch opening closed.

Outline-quilt around snow-covered roof, ribbon, windows, and door. Snip the shanks from the heart and star buttons with sharp scissors. Glue a heart button above ribbon trim to make upstairs window. Glue star button on pot holder door for knob.

Cut a 10″ length of minidot ribbon. Make a loop and tack ends to top peak of roof. Use remaining 3½″ length to tie in a bow and glue it to the top of roof over ribbon ends.

Cookie-Mold Ornaments

Ceramic cookie molds, in all their wonderful holiday shapes, produce intriguing cookies.

But the trouble with cookies is that they're so temporary. Before you've had enough time to stand back and admire your handiwork, someone has eaten it!

Here's a new use for ceramic cookie molds that produces lasting results. Don't let the photographs on the following page frighten you. The process for making these cheery cookie-mold ornaments is easier than baking cookies. And it's so much fun that the whole family will probably want to get involved.

For information on how to order ceramic cookie molds, see source listing on page 154.

Above: These Christmas tree ornaments might look like fine porcelain, but they're actually made by pressing damp bathroom tissue into ceramic cookie molds.

Materials:
1 lb. package Celluclay instant papier-mâché (or make your own)
ceramic cookie molds
vegetable oil
plain white bathroom tissue
#5 paintbrush
small container of water
#8 stencil brush
small container of water and white glue, in equal proportions
sharp craft knife
2″ length of crochet cotton or string
acrylic paints: red, green, brown
fine artists' brushes
clear acrylic spray finish
8″ (¼″-wide) satin ribbon

104

Note: Read through instructions before beginning. Make one ornament as a test.

Mix papier-mâché and set aside. Following manufacturer's instructions, coat inside of mold with vegetable oil; wipe out excess.

Place one layer of tissue in mold. Dip #5 paintbrush in water and gently tamp tissue into mold. (See Photo 1.) Allow excess tissue to extend beyond rim of mold.

Change to #8 stencil brush and continue to add additional layers of tissue, one at a time, to the mold, working slowly and carefully so as not to tear the tissue. It will not be necessary to wet the brush again before adding the second and third layers, because the tissue will absorb all the water it needs from the layers below. Wet the brush about every fourth layer, or as needed for tissue to stick to the previous layers.

After 8 layers, switch from water to the water/glue solution for added strength. At this point you can also begin working faster and tamping harder to pack tissue firmly into mold. You can even apply 2 layers at a time.

After you have built up about 18 layers, finish filling cavity of mold with papier-mâché, pressing firmly into place. (See Photo 2.) Level just to rim of mold. Wipe any excess papier-mâché away from rim, leaving edges of tissue still extending beyond rim.

Now add 8 more layers of tissue, using plain water, to cover the papier-mâché.

To remove the ornament, invert mold and rap the back several times with the back of a wooden spoon. Then turn mold over and pull ragged edges of tissue gently. (Bits of tissue may stick to mold in places as you remove the ornament. To repair ornament, simply wet the brush with plain water and tap torn edges gently in place.) Place ornament faceup on wax paper and let dry overnight. When dry to touch, turn ornament over, and let dry completely. Using sharp craft knife, trim away excess tissue, using gentle sawing motion. (See Photo 3.)

To add hanger, fold cotton string in half to make loop, lay ends on top back of ornament, and dab with white glue to hold in place. Then add 2 or 3 small pieces of wet tissue over ends of string to reinforce. Let dry.

Using fine artists' brushes, highlight details with acrylic paints. Let dry thoroughly.

Spray lightly with clear acrylic finish. Let dry. Tie ribbon hanger to loop.

Photo 1: Paintbrushes are used to dampen tissue and press it into cookie mold.

Photo 2: After applying about 18 layers of tissue, fill cavity of mold with papier-mâché.

Photo 3: When your ornament has dried completely, use a very sharp craft knife to cut away excess tissue.

Country Sheep To Cuddle

Simple garter and stockinette stitches make up these folksy knitted sheep.

Materials for one sheep:
worsted-weight yarn in the following
  amounts: 150 yards main color, 50 yards
  black
size 7 knitting needles (or size to obtain
  gauge)
stitch markers
tapestry needle
stuffing
small buttons or beads for eyes

GAUGE: 4½ sts and 9 rows = 1" in garter st.

BODY: With main color, cast on 41 sts. *Row 1:* K. *Row 2:* K 1, inc 1, k next 19 sts, place marker on needle, inc 1, k next st, inc 1, place another marker on needle, k next 19 sts, inc 1, k last st. *Rows 3, 5, 7, 9, 11, and 13:* K. *Rows 4, 6, 8, 10, 12, and 14:* Rep row 2, inc 1 st at each edge and between markers as before (69 sts after last inc). *Row 15 and following:* Work even in garter st (k every row) until piece measures 6" from beg. Dec 1 st at each edge every other row 4 times. Dec 1 st at each edge and after first and before second marker 7 times (33 sts after last dec).

Note: Last dec between markers is worked as k 2 tog, k 1, pass first st over st just k.

Work even for 2 rows.

HEAD: Change to black and St st. Dec 1 st before first marker and after second marker every other row 4 times.

Note: Sl 1, k 1, psso to work dec before first marker; k 2 tog to work dec after second marker.

Dec 1 st at each edge and at center as before, every other row 2 times. Thread yarn through rem 17 sts, pull up tightly, and tie off.

EARS: Make 2. With black, cast on 9 sts. *Rows 1 and 2:* K. *Row 3:* K 6, turn. *Row 4:* K 6. *Row 5:* K 3, turn. *Row 6:* K 3. *Row 7:* Bind off.

LEGS: Make 4. With black, cast on 12 sts.

Work even in St st for 12 rows. Thread yarn through sts, pull up tightly, and tie off.

TAIL: With main color, cast on 4 sts. Work 12 rows even in garter st. Dec 1 st at each edge. Work 1 row even. Inc 1 st at each edge. Work 12 rows even and bind off.

FINISHING: Fold body in half lengthwise, sew seam, and stuff. Fold tail piece in half, sew side seams, and sew open end to body. Sew ears to head. Sew on eyes, pulling thread firmly through head to indent eyes slightly. With main color, make rows of loops secured by backstitches on forehead. Clip loops and trim. Sew leg seams, stuff, and sew to body. With black, make 3 or 4 sts between legs to tack legs tog and keep them from spreading.

Standard Knitting Abbreviations:
beg—beginning
dec—decrease
inc—increase
k—knit
p—purl
psso—pass slipped stitch over
rem—remaining
rep—repeat
sl—slip
st(s)—stitch(es)
St st—stockinette stitch (k 1 row, p 1 row)
tog—together
"Work even" means to work in pattern stitch with no increases or decreases.

Santa Bear Is Coming to Town!

With his red cap tilted back, Santa Bear looks ready for a short nap after a long day in the elves' workshop. He'll be a favorite companion for some young elf on your list this Christmas.

Materials:
pattern on page 147
graphite paper (to transfer
 pattern to wood)
16″ pine 1 x 4
jigsaw
drill with ⅛″ bit
medium- and fine-grade sandpaper
wood sealer
tape
acrylic paints: red, raw sienna, green, white,
 burnt umber, and black
disposable palette
brushes: #4 China bristle brush, #6 square
 shader brush, #1 short liner brush
acrylic modeling paste
good-quality water-base satin varnish
1 yard red rug yarn, cut into 4 equal
 pieces
toothpicks

Transfer pattern to pine. Cut out with jigsaw. Drill holes as indicated on pattern. Sand each piece smooth with medium-grade sandpaper. Seal with wood sealer; then sand with fine-grade sandpaper when dry.

To transfer the details to the prepared wood, it is best to cut the pattern apart; then slip the graphite paper under it before taping each pattern piece to the wood. Trace the pattern with a sharp pencil.

Using #4 China bristle brush, coat each area with color indicated. Let paint dry and apply a second coat of each color if necessary. Using the same brush, lightly stipple raw sienna areas of bear (areas marked 2 on the pattern) with a mixture of white and raw sienna.

Mix approximately 2 tablespoons of modeling paste with a few drops of white acrylic paint. Apply this mixture over all the white areas with the China bristle brush. Stipple the areas with the same brush to get the desired texture for trim. Wet the shader brush; using the corner, paint a thin blush of red over the cheeks. Using the liner brush, paint the eyes burnt umber; then add black centers. When paint is dry, add white highlight dots. Paint the nose black; then add a white highlight dot. Use burnt umber for bear's mouth.

When the paint is dry, apply several coats of varnish, allowing to dry between coats.

Use a toothpick to push the yarn through the holes in the arms, legs, and body. Tie yarn together on the back of bear.

Holiday Greetings
With Shadow-Quilted Cards

If you like old-fashioned needlework, you'll love these cards. They combine appliqué, quilting, and embroidery.

Sunbonnet Sue

Materials:
pattern on page 153
tracing paper
#3 lead pencil
4" x 6" piece of muslin
4" x 6" piece of white voile, organdy, or organza
scraps of solid red, red miniprint, black, green, peach fabrics
matching thread
fabric glue stick
quilting needle
embroidery needle
red, green embroidery flosses
purchased window card or any greeting card with framed design
4" x 6" piece of white paper

Rocking Horse

Materials:
pattern on page 153
tracing paper
#3 lead pencil
5" x 7" piece of muslin
5" x 7" piece of white voile, organdy, or organza
scraps of light brown, red pindot, green miniprint fabrics
matching thread
fabric glue stick
quilting needle
embroidery needle
red, black, brown embroidery flosses
purchased window card or any greeting card with framed design
5" x 7" piece of white paper

Christmas Tree

Materials:
pattern on page 153
tracing paper
#3 lead pencil
4" x 5" piece of white fabric
4" x 5" piece of white voile, organdy, or organza
4" x 5" piece of green fabric
green thread
fabric glue stick
quilting needle
embroidery needle
white, red, green embroidery flosses
gold metallic thread
purchased window card or any greeting card with framed design
4" x 5" piece of white paper

Trace patterns onto tracing paper. Cut out each piece along traced edge, cutting away pencil mark. With glue stick, glue right side of tracing paper pieces to wrong side of fabric scraps, using colors indicated on patterns. Cut out each piece with no seam allowance.

Trace the entire design onto muslin background fabric. Glue the colored pieces in place on the background fabric. (Leave tracing paper on back of pieces to add stability.)

Place voile piece on top of design. Pin or baste all layers together. Using matching thread and starting at the center to avoid shifting of design, quilt around edges of all pattern pieces. Add embroidered details as shown on pattern. Embroider your initials on design, if desired.

If greeting card with framed design is used, carefully cut out framed design, leaving window in center of card. Center completed design in cut-out window of card. Glue design in place. Glue the white paper to the back of design.

Opposite: To make these holiday cards, solid-colored or print fabrics, which form the design, are sandwiched between a bottom layer of lightweight fabric and a top layer of sheer material, such as organza or voile.

Ideas

These Paper Crafts Are Child's Play

If you have the job of entertaining out-of-school youngsters through endless winter days, here's some help. These projects will keep your children happy for hours.

Above: Simple paper crafts help keep little hands busy throughout Christmas vacation. These activities also let children contribute to the fun and excitement of your family's holiday decorating.

● Use cookie cutters or shapes traced from books and magazines to make yards of paper doll garlands. Fold paper into an accordion the exact width of your shape. Trace the shape onto the front of the folded paper; then cut around the shape through all thicknesses of paper, leaving one small area on each side of the shape uncut. (See Diagram 1.)

○ For each paper lantern, cut a rectangle from craft paper or holiday wrapping paper. Fold in half lengthwise. Cut slits on folded side as shown in Diagram 2. Unfold the paper and bend it into a circle, overlapping the ends. Glue or staple ends. (See Diagram 3.) Punch holes opposite each other in the top edge. Knot one end of a piece of cord or ribbon and thread through both holes; then knot other end.

● For pretty spiral ornaments, start with circles of brightly colored paper. Following Diagram 4, start cutting at outer edge and continue cutting around and around until you reach center of circle. Punch a hole in center of circle and tie a piece of string through it for a hanger.

● To make a lacy wonderland of paper snowflakes, fold squares of white paper into 8ths. Make random cuts in paper. (See Diagram 5.) Unfold paper to a delicate snowy surprise.

○ A few sheets of construction paper or colored magazine pages and a handheld hole punch will keep children busy making confetti.

● Paper chains are never out of date. For a change from the familiar construction paper kind, let your child experiment with different materials, such as Christmas wrap, paper craft ribbon, or origami paper.

Diagram 1 – Garland

Cutting line

Do not cut on fold

Diagram 2 – Lantern

Cutting line

Fold line

Diagram 3 – Lantern

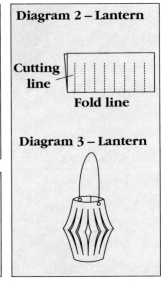

Diagram 4– Spiral

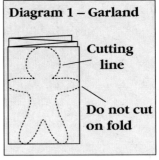

String

Cutting line

Diagram 5 – Snowflake

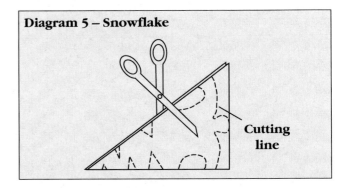

Cutting line

Above: A roll of plain brown wrapping paper and a few simple shapes are all your child needs to make rows and rows of paper doll garland for the tree, mantel, or doors and windows.

Above: Miniature lanterns, snaky spirals, and paper chains make festive tree ornaments; and making them is a lot of fun. Background: Just like the real thing, no two paper snowflakes are identical. Maybe that's why generations of youngsters have found hours of entertainment in cutting them.

Pleasures of the Season

A HO-HO HAPPY
BIRTHDAY

FIRESIDE CHEER

CHRISTMAS AT A COUNTRY INN

WOW! A KITCHEN PARTY
FOR KIDS!

IDEAS: HOLIDAY FOR
THE BIRDS

A Ho-Ho-Happy Birthday

"We bring the Santas down from the attic, and I get reacquainted with each one," says Judy.

Nearly a quarter of a century ago, Judy Murtagh's husband, David, gave her a Santa Claus. One single papier-mâché Santa. Judy's birthday is December 21, so she was used to receiving Christmas things on her special day. She liked the little Santa a lot and decided to collect a few more. That first Santa now has the company of close to 400 others.

Christmas begins early for the Murtagh family. The week before Thanksgiving, boxes are carried down from the attic—boxes and more boxes filled with generations of Santa Clauses.

"It takes about five weeks to complete the decorating," Judy admits. "To arrange the Santas a different way from the year before takes quite awhile."

Judy's real impetus for decorating early is her birthday party. A Christmas enthusiast all her life, Judy makes her birthday the introduction to the season. Her entire home is decorated, Santas inhabiting every room, just in time for the party. Family members are invited for dinner and to decorate the Murtagh's 16-foot Christmas tree, which stands in the entrance to their historic home in West Chester, Pennsylvania.

"I put a pot of soup on the open fire," Judy says. "When my family arrives—aunts, uncles, and cousins—I give each one two boxes of ornaments. They don't get to eat until the tree is finished. Sometimes I find a few boxes hidden under the couch when everyone is gone."

Right: A four-foot-tall Father Christmas warms himself by the blazing fire. Handcrafted by artist Sara Baker in 1987, he is proof that Judy always purchases a Santa for the expression on his face.

Judy's second hobby is open-hearth cooking. In the winter months, she keeps a pot of soup simmering over the fire. The stone hearth was built in 1783.

114

For her birthday, Judy can always expect a few new Santas to add to her collection. She unwraps Santas at Christmas, Easter, and even Mother's Day. She appreciates both the antique and the reproduction Santas, but admits that the detail and care put into some of the newer handcrafted Santas make them especially dear.

"I always look at the face first," Judy confides. "If I like the expression, then I want it."

Each jolly old elf must give Judy a wink of an eye and see right into her heart. In the Murtagh collection, there's always room for one more Santa.

Above: This 1976 addition to the Murtagh's home, which was built in 1705, offers a grand view of their Echo Valley Farm. The room is honored by the Santa tree, decorated exclusively with Santa ornaments Judy has collected over the years. The largest jolly old elf was originally used in a Christmas store display.

Bottom right: A hand-painted tin Santa on the mantel contemplates his pipe as he looks over a gathering of old and reproduction Santas. Yarrow, cockscomb, dried pomegranates, and nosegays of assorted dried flowers accentuate a tree decked out in American flags.

Below: In Germany, St. Nicholas became known as Pelze Nicol, *the fur clad Nicholas Hero, bundled in fur hat and cape, his face, hands, and feet are molded from clay; his beard is made from fine flax.*

Left: Until the 14th century, St. Nicholas had a black beard. It changed to white as the Santa legend blended with an even older one, involving a pagan god, Odin. He rode through the night skies at the winter solstice on a white horse, his white beard flowing. Children would fill their shoes on the steps with carrots and hay for his horse. It was at this time, during his mid-European visits, that St. Nick acquired a white beard and white horse.

Above: Another handcrafted reproduction, this St. Nicholas is robed in rich velvets and furs.

117

Fireside Cheer

Outside, old December may be putting on a show with his howling winds and falling temperatures, decorating his holiday landscape with icicles and snow. But inside, you and your family will be cozy warm as you celebrate beside a crackling fire.

Here are some dishes just made for fireside festivities. Intriguing spice-laden drinks, like Fireside Wassail and Spiced Fruit Nog, kick off the holiday cheer. And hearty Beef Stew en Croûte, Potato-Green Bean Casserole, and Cabbage Patch Coleslaw satisfy the appetite.

Ruby Apples with Custard Sauce makes a perfect dessert for this fireside feast. In fact, if you're feeling adventurous, you might forego the oven when preparing these luscious baked apples. Instead, after you've cored and stuffed them, wrap them in heavy aluminum foil and bury them in the hot fireplace ashes for an hour or so.

Spiced Fruit Nog

12 eggs, separated
1 cup sugar
½ teaspoon ground nutmeg
¼ teaspoon ground cinnamon
¼ teaspoon ground allspice
2 cups apricot nectar
2 cups half-and-half
1 (12-ounce) can evaporated milk
2 teaspoons rum flavoring
Grated orange rind (optional)

Combine egg yolks, sugar, and spices in top of a double boiler. Place over simmering water and cook, stirring constantly with a wire whisk, until mixture reaches 165°. Remove from heat and cool to room temperature.

Combine yolk mixture, egg whites, apricot nectar, half-and-half, evaporated milk, and rum flavoring; beat at medium speed of an electric mixer until well blended. Cover and refrigerate until thoroughly chilled. Pour chilled nog into serving cups and sprinkle with orange rind, if desired. Yield: 2 quarts.

Potato-Green Bean Casserole

1 large onion, chopped
2 large cloves garlic, minced
¼ cup plus 1½ teaspoons butter or margarine, melted
¼ cup plus 1½ teaspoons all-purpose flour
1½ cups half-and-half
1 cup (4 ounces) shredded Monterey Jack cheese
¾ cup Chablis or other dry white wine
1¼ teaspoons salt
½ teaspoon white pepper
4 small baking potatoes, unpeeled and cut into ¼-inch slices (about 1½ pounds)
1 (9-ounce) package frozen cut green beans, thawed
½ cup grated Parmesan cheese
1 (7¼-ounce) jar roasted red peppers, drained

Sauté onion and garlic in melted butter in a large saucepan until tender. Add flour, stirring well; cook 1 minute, stirring constantly. Gradually add half-and-half; cook over medium heat, stirring constantly, until mixture is thickened and bubbly. Add Monterey Jack cheese, stirring until melted. Remove from heat and stir in wine, salt, and pepper. Set aside.

Layer half of potato slices and half of green beans in a lightly greased 12- x 8- x 2-inch baking dish. Spoon half of cheese sauce over top; sprinkle with Parmesan cheese. Repeat layers with remaining potato slices, green beans, and cheese sauce. Cover and bake at 375° for 1 hour and 15 minutes or until potatoes are tender.

Lay roasted peppers out flat on a paper towel-lined surface. Cut out each pepper with a festive 1-inch cookie cutter and arrange on top of casserole. Serve hot. Yield: 8 servings.

Note: You can roast your own sweet red peppers for use on top of Potato-Green Bean Casserole by following directions for Gift-Givers' Roasted Peppers, found on page 36. If roasted peppers will be used immediately, you may omit the canning process.

Opposite: As the yule log burns, serve your family and friends some spicy treats, like Ruby Apples with Custard Sauce and Fireside Wassail.

Beef Stew en Croûte

1¾ pounds beef stew meat, cut into 1-inch cubes
2 cloves garlic, chopped
2 tablespoons vegetable oil
2 (12-ounce) jars commercial brown gravy
1 (14½-ounce) can whole tomatoes, undrained and chopped
¼ cup tomato paste
1 tablespoon Worcestershire sauce
2 bay leaves
1 teaspoon dried whole thyme
¼ teaspoon salt
⅛ teaspoon pepper
3 medium carrots, scraped and cut into ½-inch slices
2 small onions, cut into eighths
¼ pound fresh mushrooms, halved
3 tablespoons chopped fresh parsley
1 (17¼-ounce) package frozen puff pastry, thawed
1 egg, beaten
1 tablespoon water

Brown meat and garlic in hot oil in an oven-proof Dutch oven; drain off pan drippings. Add gravy and next 7 ingredients to Dutch oven, stirring well. Cover and bake at 350° for 30 minutes. Add carrots to meat mixture; cover and bake an additional 30 minutes. Add onions, mushrooms, and parsley; continue to bake, covered, 30 minutes or until meat and vegetables are tender. Remove and discard bay leaves. Ladle stew into eight 10-ounce ovenproof bowls or ramekins.

Roll puff pastry sheets to ⅛-inch thickness on a lightly floured surface. Cut out 8 pastry rounds, 1 inch larger than circumference of top of each bowl, using a sharp knife. Cut 8 small holly leaf shapes from scraps of puff pastry and set aside.

Combine egg and water, stirring until well blended. With half of egg mixture, evenly brush 1 side of pastry rounds; set remaining egg mixture aside. Place pastry rounds, egg mixture side down, over each bowl; press pastry firmly against top edges of bowl, using the tines of a fork to seal edges. Refrigerate 30 minutes to set pastry.

Evenly brush tops of pastry rounds with remaining egg mixture; place a pastry holly leaf on top of each serving and brush lightly with egg mixture. Bake at 450° for 10 minutes or until pastry is puffed and golden brown. Serve hot. Yield: 8 servings.

Cabbage Patch Coleslaw

2½ cups shredded green cabbage
1 cup shredded red cabbage
½ cup thinly sliced carrot
½ cup chopped sweet red pepper
½ cup chopped green pepper
¼ cup chopped onion
2 tablespoons chopped fresh parsley
⅓ cup vinegar
⅓ cup commercial Italian salad dressing
⅓ cup sugar
⅛ teaspoon salt
Dash of pepper
2 medium-size sweet red peppers
2 medium-size green peppers

Combine first 7 ingredients in a large bowl, tossing well. Combine vinegar, salad dressing, sugar, salt, and pepper in a small jar; cover tightly with lid and shake vigorously. Pour dressing mixture over vegetables and toss gently to coat well. Cover and refrigerate until thoroughly chilled.

Cut red and green peppers in half lengthwise; remove membranes and seeds, leaving stems intact. Rinse thoroughly under cold water and invert on paper towels to drain. Cut a thin slice from bottom of each pepper half so it will sit upright. Toss coleslaw and spoon evenly into pepper cups, using a slotted spoon. Arrange pepper cups on a serving platter. Yield: 8 servings.

Fireside Wassail

12 whole cloves
2 (3-inch) sticks cinnamon
2 quarts apple cider
2 cups pineapple juice
2 cups orange juice
¾ cup lemon juice
½ cup sugar
Cinnamon sticks (optional)
Lemon slices (optional)
Whole cloves (optional)

120

Tie 12 cloves and 2 cinnamon sticks in a cheesecloth bag. Combine spice bag, apple cider, juices, and sugar in a Dutch oven, stirring well; cover and bring to a boil. Reduce heat and simmer for 30 minutes. Discard the spice bag.

Pour wassail into serving mugs and serve hot. If desired, garnish each serving with a cinnamon stick and a lemon slice studded with whole cloves. Yield: about 3 quarts.

Ruby Apples with Custard Sauce

8 medium-size red cooking apples
¼ cup plus 2 tablespoons firmly packed brown sugar
1 tablespoon plus 1½ teaspoons all-purpose flour
1½ teaspoons ground cinnamon
2 tablespoons plus 1½ teaspoons butter or margarine
⅓ cup raisins
2 tablespoons finely chopped pecans
Custard Sauce (recipe follows)
Freshly grated nutmeg (optional)

Core each apple to within ½ inch from bottom. Combine brown sugar, flour, and cinnamon in a small bowl; cut in butter, using a pastry blender, until mixture resembles coarse meal. Stir in raisins and pecans. Spoon brown sugar mixture evenly into cavities of apples.

Place apples in a 13- x 9- x 2-inch baking dish. Cover and bake at 350° for 1 hour. Dollop Custard Sauce on top of each apple. Sprinkle with nutmeg, if desired. Yield: 8 servings.

Custard Sauce:

4 egg yolks
½ cup sugar
Dash of salt
½ cup sherry
1 tablespoon applejack brandy
2 teaspoons lemon juice
1 cup whipping cream, whipped

Combine egg yolks, sugar, and salt in top of a double boiler, beating well with a wire whisk. Gradually stir in sherry, applejack brandy, and lemon juice. Place over simmering water and

cook, stirring constantly with wire whisk, until mixture thickens. Remove from heat. Cool to room temperature; cover and refrigerate until thoroughly chilled. Fold whipped cream into chilled mixture and serve. Yield: about 2 cups.

Stuffed Calico Apples

A basket of these calico apples will make a festive country centerpiece.

Materials for one large and one small apple:
patterns on page 152
10″ square of red print fabric (for large apple)
8″ square of red print fabric (for small apple)
stuffing
scraps of green print fabric (for leaves)
thread to match
1½″ (¼″-diameter) wooden dowel (for stem of large apple)
1″ (¼″-diameter) wooden dowel (for stem of small apple)
craft glue
long needle
carpet thread

For each apple, fold red print fabric in half with right sides facing; transfer pattern and cut out. Keeping fabric folded, stitch outer edges together. For inner edges, unfold fabric and bring lobes together. Stitch left side of right lobe to right side of left lobe, and vice versa. Clip curves; turn. Stuff fully; stitch opening closed.

Transfer leaf pattern to green print fabric 4 times and cut out. With right sides facing, stitch 2 leaf pieces together, leaving straight edge open. Clip curves and turn. Stuff leaf. Repeat with remaining 2 leaf pieces.

Cut one end of the dowel on a diagonal. Glue one leaf around the flat end of dowel. Glue remaining leaf to opposite side of dowel; let dry.

Thread long needle with carpet thread. Take 3 stitches through center of apple from top to bottom, pulling tightly each time to shape apple.

Glue stem and leaves in center of apple top.

121

Calico Apple Coasters

Materials for one coaster:
patterns on page 153
scrap of brown print fabric (for stem)
scrap of green print fabric (for leaf)
5½″ x 10½″ piece of red print fabric (for apple)
5½″ square of fleece
thread to match

Fold brown print fabric in half lengthwise with right sides facing. Transfer pattern for stem to print fabric and cut out. Keeping fabric folded, stitch together, leaving ends open. Turn and press. Transfer pattern for leaf to green print fabric twice and cut out. With right sides facing, stitch pieces together, leaving straight edge open. Turn and press.

Fold red print fabric in half. Transfer pattern for apple to folded red print fabric and cut out. Transfer pattern for apple to fleece and cut out. Lay one apple piece, right side up, on top of fleece piece and pin. Fold stem in half with ends even. Pin to apple where indicated on pattern, with stem fold toward bottom. Lay the second apple fabric piece on top of the first with right sides facing. Stitch together, leaving open where indicated. Clip curves and turn.

Fold in raw edges of apple and slip the leaf between the layers beside the stem. Stitch the opening closed, catching the leaf with a few stitches to secure.

Topstitch ¼″ from edge all around the apple.

Below: Baskets of stuffed calico apples and calico apple coasters make a great country accompaniment to your fireside gathering.

Christmas at a Country Inn

Above: The tables are set and the fire is blazing. The Silver Leaf Country Inn is ready to receive holiday visitors. A handmade dulcimer rests on a bench beside the fireplace, and a tall Tennessee cedar, filled with handmade ornaments, stands in the corner. A photograph of the inn's exterior hangs on the wall beside the fireplace.

It's a Sunday afternoon in mid-December on a hill above a creek in middle Tennessee. Greenery and red bows decorate the split-rail fence beside the pathway leading to a big log house that was built almost 175 years ago. Pine and cedar garlands and wreaths hang at every door and window.

As one enters the Silver Leaf Country Inn, the aroma of roast pork and the sweet old-fashioned smells of jam cake and boiled custard assail the senses. Guests, waiting for their tables, sit or stand beside a massive stone fireplace, munching hot parched peanuts and tossing the hulls into the fire. Christmas carols—played in the traditional Tennessee style on dulcimers, banjos, and fiddles—mingle with talk and laughter. Tall cedars, their limbs loaded with handmade ornaments, stand in every room.

123

From tables inside the three dining rooms, visitors look out into the surrounding woodlands. Myriads of songbirds—including chickadees, titmice, and cardinals—feast at the feeders that innkeepers Norma and Johnny Crow have placed about the grounds. Occasionally, a white-tailed deer can be seen at the edge of the woods.

And so it has been since the late seventies when the Crows purchased the house, one of the oldest in Tennessee, and moved it to its present site near their home. Both former state senators, Norma and Johnny were already accustomed to serving people. And with Norma's cooking talents and love for all things old, the inn was a natural step for them.

"My dream was to have a country inn," says Norma, "to make every guest feel at home and to serve them the best in home-style cooking."

Her dream came true. Not just at Christmastime, but all through the year, the food at the Silver Leaf is worth writing home about. And the gracious Tennessee hospitality is another reason guests return time and again.

Norma, along with a talented kitchen staff, does the cooking, using many time-tested family recipes. She makes all her own jams, jellies, and preserves with fruit from the Crow farm.

Although the food is the shining star of the Silver Leaf Country Inn, many visitors also choose to stay overnight or spend an entire weekend in one of the inn's homey guest rooms. They find the countryside is a good place to unwind, relax, and do nothing—an especially appealing activity in the thick of the Christmas rush.

Perhaps you and your family might enjoy this type of quiet retreat this Christmas. Whether for lunch and an afternoon stroll or for a peace-filled weekend, a respite in the country can rest your soul, renew your spirits, and get you ready for that final burst of Christmas merry-making.

But if your schedule won't allow you the luxury of a trip to a country inn, at least you can sample some inn-style food. Try the following recipe for Norma's Orange-Raisin Bran Muffins. Serve them hot with butter, jam, coffee, and perhaps some fresh fruit or fruit juice, for a breakfast or brunch that will put you in the country Christmas spirit.

For more information about accommodations at the Silver Leaf Inn, see page 154. Contact your state's tourism division for a list of country inns near you.

Norma's Orange-Raisin Bran Muffins

3½ cups wheat bran flakes cereal with raisins
1½ cups buttermilk
½ cup frozen orange juice concentrate, thawed and undiluted
½ cup vegetable oil
2 eggs, beaten
2½ cups all-purpose flour
1½ cups sugar
2½ teaspoons baking soda
1 teaspoon salt

Combine first 5 ingredients, stirring well; let stand 5 minutes.

Combine flour, sugar, soda, and salt in a large bowl; make a well in center of mixture. Add cereal mixture, stirring just until moistened. Cover batter and store in refrigerator up to 6 weeks.

When ready to bake, spoon batter into greased muffin pans, filling two-thirds full. Bake at 375° for 14 minutes. Remove from pans immediately. Yield: 2½ dozen.

Before You Go . . .

Country inns are famous for coziness and charm. But don't expect the amenities of a large hotel. Consider these points when planning a visit to a country inn.

Most small inns have only a few guest rooms. Make reservations as early as possible. Many inns welcome children, but some do not.

Even fewer accept pets. Ask, if you plan to take either. You might also want to ask about rules for smoking and alcohol.

Some innkeepers don't accept credit cards or personal checks. Ask, before assuming your room will have a private bath, phone, or television. Knowing the rules beforehand can make your country weekend a special holiday memory.

Wow! A Kitchen Party for Kids!

School's out! The Christmas season is officially under way. It's a magical time for children—a time for fun and memory making.

To help your children or grandchildren have fun and make memories, plan a party. Hold it in the kitchen, where cleanup is easy. Serve lots of goodies that children love. And let them help prepare the treats.

The recipes that begin on this page are made to order for a kitchen party for kids. With a little adult help, the youngsters will have a blast preparing Brownie-Mint Sundae Sandwiches, Banana-Peanut Loaves, Cookie Party Pizzas, and Kid-Style Marzipan Fruit. To wash all these tasty morsels down, let the kids mix up their own glasses full of bubbly Cherry Berry Bounce.

Above: Provide your partying youngsters with bowls of chocolate and butterscotch morsels, flaked coconut, chopped nuts, and maraschino cherries and watch them build their own Cookie Party Pizzas.

Cherry Berry Bounce

1 cup unsweetened apple-cherry juice, chilled
1 teaspoon sugar
½ teaspoon cream of tartar
¼ teaspoon baking soda
1 red maraschino cherry with stem (optional)

Combine first 4 ingredients in a tall glass; stir until soda dissolves and mixture is bubbly. Serve immediately. Garnish with a cherry, if desired. Yield: 1 serving.

Banana-Peanut Loaves

1¾ cups all-purpose flour
¾ cup sugar
¾ cup chopped salted peanuts
1¼ teaspoons cream of tartar
¾ teaspoon baking soda
½ teaspoon salt
2 eggs, beaten
½ cup vegetable oil
2 ripe bananas, mashed
Creamy peanut butter (optional)

Combine all-purpose flour, sugar, salted peanuts, cream of tartar, baking soda, and salt in a large mixing bowl; make a well in the center of the mixture. Combine eggs, oil, and mashed bananas; add to the dry mixture, stirring until moistened.

Spoon batter evenly into 4 greased 5¾- x 3- x 2-inch loaf pans. Bake at 350° for 30 minutes or until a wooden toothpick inserted in center comes out clean. Cool in pans 10 minutes; remove from pans and let cool on wire racks. Slice and serve with peanut butter, if desired. Yield: 4 loaves.

Brownie-Mint Sundae Sandwiches

4 (1-ounce) squares semisweet chocolate
1 cup butter or margarine
4 eggs
2 cups sugar
1 cup all-purpose flour
¼ teaspoon salt
1 cup finely chopped walnuts, toasted
1 quart peppermint or mint-chocolate chip
  ice cream, slightly softened
Mint-Fudge Sauce (recipe follows)
Red maraschino cherries (optional)
Fresh mint sprigs (optional)

Combine semisweet chocolate and butter in top of a double boiler. Place over simmering water and cook, stirring frequently, until chocolate melts. Remove from heat and let stand 10 minutes.

Beat eggs in a large bowl at medium speed of an electric mixer until thick and lemon colored; gradually add sugar, beating well. Combine flour and salt, stirring well; add to egg mixture with chocolate mixture and beat at low speed 1 minute. Fold in walnuts.

Heavily grease two 9-inch square pans. Line bottom of pans with wax paper; grease wax paper. Spread batter evenly into prepared pans. Bake at 350° for 20 to 25 minutes or until a wooden toothpick inserted in center comes out clean. Loosen brownies from sides of pans, using a narrow metal spatula; invert onto wire racks and peel off wax paper. Cool brownies completely and wrap in heavy-duty plastic wrap. Refrigerate 8 hours or until thoroughly chilled.

Line a 9-inch square pan with heavy-duty plastic wrap, leaving a 1-inch overhang around edges. Pack ice cream into pan, spreading evenly to smooth top. Cover and freeze 8 hours or until firm.

Prepare Mint-Fudge Sauce and set aside.

To soften slightly, remove ice-cream layer from freezer and from pan 5 minutes before assembling sandwich. Remove plastic wrap from ice-cream and brownie layers. Place ice-cream layer on 1 brownie layer; top with remaining brownie layer. Press sandwich together gently, making layers adhere; cut into 3-inch squares, using a warm knife. Transfer sandwiches to serving plates and top with Mint-Fudge Sauce; serve immediately. If desired, garnish each serving with cherries and mint. Yield: 9 servings.

Mint-Fudge Sauce:

⅔ cup mint chocolate morsels
3 tablespoons butter or margarine
1¼ cups sifted powdered sugar
1 (5-ounce) can evaporated milk

Combine chocolate morsels and butter in top of a double boiler; place over simmering water and cook, stirring frequently, until chocolate melts. Gradually add powdered sugar and milk. Continue to cook, stirring constantly, 5 minutes or until thickened. Remove from heat and let cool at least 10 minutes before serving. Yield: about 1½ cups.

Cookie Party Pizzas

1 (20-ounce) roll refrigerated peanut butter
  cookie dough
1½ cups marshmallow cream
1 cup semisweet chocolate mini-morsels
½ cup flaked coconut
¼ cup red maraschino cherries, sliced
¼ cup green maraschino cherries, sliced
½ cup coarsely chopped pecans, toasted
1 cup caramel topping
1 cup butterscotch morsels
1 cup butter-brickle chips
½ cup coarsely chopped salted peanuts
2 (1-ounce) squares semisweet chocolate

Divide cookie dough into 4 equal portions. Pat each portion into an 8-inch circle on lightly greased baking sheets, using lightly greased fingers. Bake at 350° for 8 to 10 minutes. Carefully remove from baking sheets and cool on wire racks.

Spread marshmallow cream evenly over surface of 2 cookie pizzas; sprinkle evenly with mini-morsels, coconut, cherries, and pecans. Spread caramel topping evenly over surface of remaining 2 cookie pizzas; sprinkle evenly with butterscotch morsels, butter-brickle chips, and peanuts.

Place chocolate in top of a double boiler. Place over simmering water and cook, stirring frequently, until chocolate melts; drizzle over caramel-topped cookie pizzas. Cut cookie pizzas into wedges to serve. Yield: four 8-inch cookie pizzas.

Note: Cookie Party Pizzas can be packaged for gift giving. Place each on an 8-inch cardboard round and present in a lightweight cardboard pie box (available from local bakeries).

Kid-Style Marzipan Fruit

2 (8-ounce) cans almond paste
¼ cup light corn syrup
1 teaspoon almond extract
3 cups sifted powdered sugar
Red, yellow, green, blue liquid food
   coloring
2 egg whites, lightly beaten
2 tablespoons strawberry-flavored gelatin
1 (3-inch) stick cinnamon
Currants
Whole cloves
Licorice

Knead almond paste by hand in a large bowl. Add corn syrup and almond extract; knead into almond paste. Gradually knead in powdered sugar, 1 cup at a time, allowing dough to rest after each addition. Divide marzipan dough into 5 portions. Tint 2 portions with red food coloring, 2 with yellow, and 1 with green, using about ⅛ teaspoon food coloring for each. Knead each portion until food coloring is well blended into dough. Add blue food coloring, 1 drop at a time, to 1 portion of red marzipan dough to make dough purple. Add red food coloring, 1 drop at a time, to 1 portion of yellow marzipan dough to make dough orange. Knead dough until desired color is reached.

Follow directions below to shape marzipan dough, working with 1 or 2 portions at a time. Wrap remaining portions in plastic wrap and let stand at room temperature until ready to shape.

Leaves: Roll half of green dough to ⅛-inch thickness on wax paper. Cut dough into leaves with a cookie or canapé cutter. Draw leaf indentations, using a wooden toothpick.

Strawberries: Shape one-third of red dough into 8 small balls. Shape a rounded point at 1 end of each ball and slightly flatten opposite end. Slightly indent flattened ends, using the end of a spoon handle. Brush each strawberry with egg white and roll in strawberry-flavored gelatin; transfer to wax paper to dry. Press several leaves into indentation in each flattened end.

Apples: Mold one-third of red dough into 3 balls, stretching each to form an apple shape. Break cinnamon stick into small splinters; insert a splinter into each ball for stem. Press several leaves into dough around each stem.

Watermelons: Mold remaining one-third of red dough into 3 ovals. Flatten remaining half of green dough to make skins for watermelons. Gently mold green dough around red ovals; pinch each seam to seal and smooth with fingers. Cut melons in half lengthwise. Arrange currants on cut surfaces to resemble seeds.

Peaches: Shape half of yellow dough into 4 balls. Insert a whole clove, head down, into top of each peach, leaving pointed end out for stem. Press several leaves into dough around each stem. Press a groove on 1 side of each peach, using a wooden toothpick. Combine 2 tablespoons water, 2 drops yellow, and 2 drops red food coloring. Lightly brush over sides of peach to tint; transfer to wax paper to dry.

Bananas: Mold remaining half of yellow dough into 6 banana shapes. Insert a whole clove, head up, into each banana at stem end.

Grapes: Shape purple dough into small balls to make 5 clusters of grapes. Brush balls with egg white, gently pressing them together to form clusters; transfer to wax paper to dry. Push a ¼-inch piece of licorice into stem end of each cluster. Press several leaves into dough around each stem.

Oranges: Shape half of orange dough into 4 balls. Roll each orange over a grater to obtain a rough skin. Insert a whole clove, head up, into each orange at stem end.

Pumpkins: Form remaining half of orange dough into 3 balls. Lightly score 5 vertical indentations around each pumpkin, using a wooden toothpick. Insert a whole clove, head down, into top of each pumpkin, leaving pointed end out for stem.

Gently brush marzipan fruit with egg white to achieve a shiny surface. Transfer to wax paper and let stand at room temperature at least 30 minutes to dry. Serve marzipan fruit in miniature paper muffin cups. Store in refrigerator in an airtight container. Yield: about 3½ dozen.

Note: Marzipan dough can be wrapped in heavy-duty plastic wrap and refrigerated in an airtight container up to 2 weeks. Let dough reach room temperature before shaping.

A Christmas Teddy Sweatshirt

What's the proper dress for a kid to wear to a Christmas party in the kitchen? A sweatshirt featuring an appliquéd teddy bear with a Christmas bib.

Materials:
pattern on pages 150 and 151
tracing paper
⅓ yard (36"- or 45"-wide) medium brown pindot fabric
4" x 8" scrap of light brown pindot fabric
3" x 8" scrap of white fabric with red polka dots
3" x 18" scrap of red-and-white calico
12" x 20" piece of fleece for batting
1" square of brown felt
water-soluble marker
matching thread
red acrylic paint
liner paintbrush
12" (½"-wide) red rickrack
9" (18"-wide) red satin ribbon
2 (½") black buttons
white sweatshirt

Transfer pattern to tracing paper. Pin pattern to fabrics and cut out pieces as indicated. Transfer all pattern markings to fabric with the water-soluble marker.

Place fabric bear body pieces with right sides facing. Place fleece body piece on top of these. Pin or baste through all layers of fabric. Sew, leaving bottom open as indicated. Clip curves and turn, leaving fleece on inside. Press. Slipstitch the opening closed.

Place muzzle on bear and satin-stitch (short, close zigzag stitch) in place by machine. Stitch paddies and paw pad on the bear in the same manner.

Place the fabric hind foot pieces with right sides facing. Place the fleece foot piece on the top of these. Pin or baste through all layers of fabric. Sew completely around foot. Clip curves. Cut a 3" slash in the back of foot where indicated. Turn through slash, leaving fleece inside. Press. Slipstitch slash closed. Satin-stitch the toes and foot pads in place by machine.

With the red paint and the liner brush, paint words on bib. Let paint dry. Sew bib to front of bear where indicated. Zigzag-stitch rickrack around bottom of bib and ribbon across top edge of bib.

Satin-stitch cheeks, mouth, and nose to bear's face where indicated. Satin-stitch line from bottom of nose to mouth as indicated. Hand-sew button eyes in place. Satin-stitch the ears where indicated.

With right sides facing, stitch tie pieces, leaving open where indicated. Clip corners, turn, and press.

Slipstitch opening closed. Tie knot in center of tie and tack in place at top right corner of bib. Place hind feet on front of the bear and tack in place at center back of each foot through back layer only.

Center finished bear on the front of white sweatshirt. Pin. Slipstitch the bear to the shirt along outline of bear, leaving tie and hind feet free.

Care instructions: Turn the shirt wrong side out and machine-wash in cold water. Do not use chlorine bleach. Line dry.

Left: With his bright red bandanna tie and big floppy bear feet, this teddy is ready for fun, as his friend enjoys a glass of Cherry Berry Bounce (recipe on page 125).

Letters to Santa

Once again, the writing tablets are spread out on the kitchen table, where the children are hard at work. Every hope and desire is being conjured up.

All the wishes of a child's entire year can be summed up in the treasured letters sent to the old man at the North Pole. Here's a way to save those cherished words for Christmases to come.

You can make those precious letters into ornaments—sturdy cardboard-backed letters that will add the innocence of childhood wherever they hang. And you'll be reminded from year to year of your child's favorite things.

If you don't have quite enough real letters, or if they must be mailed to the North Pole, use your childhood memories to make up a few. You'll get the spirit across.

Materials for one ornament:
scrap of ⅛″-thick plywood
band saw
sandpaper
sheet from a primary school writing tablet
white glue
drill with ¼″ bit
black medium-point permanent pen
8″ (⅛″-wide) red ribbon

Using the saw, cut a 3″ x 4″ rectangle out of wood. (Use a 3″ heart-shaped cookie cutter as a pattern for variety.) Sand edges. Using the wood as a pattern, trace shape onto paper. With black pen, let your child write a short note to Santa, keeping inside cutting lines. Or compose a note yourself, using a child-like script. Cut out shape and glue to wood. Allow to dry. Drill 2 (¼″) holes near top, referring to photograph for placement. Tie ribbon through holes for hanger.

129

Cozy Sweatshirts For Christmas Fun

These decorated sweatshirts will show your Christmas spirit all through the holidays.

Angel Cardigan Sweatshirt

Materials:
stencil pattern on page 145
red cotton sweatshirt
1½ yards white cotton-knit binding
thread to match
mylar template material
sharp craft knife
white fabric paint
small stencil brush
2 yards (⅛" wide) white satin ribbon

Wash and dry sweatshirt. Using a ruler and pencil, make a mark down center front of shirt from neck opening to bottom of band. Cut sweatshirt front along this line.

Carefully separate the 2 layers of bottom band and cut along bottom fold. Then cut off inner layer close to seam line. Trim band to 1½". Turn under ¼" of band and then turn band under to make hem. Stitch hem to shirt.

Cut 2 pieces of binding the length of the center front opening plus ½". With right sides facing, pin binding to one side of shirt opening, allowing binding to extend ¼" at top and bottom of shirt. Machine-stitch binding to shirt, using a ¼" seam. Turn binding to inside of shirt and slipstitch, tucking under ¼" along front edge and at top and bottom. Repeat for second side of shirt opening.

Transfer stencil pattern to mylar. Using sharp craft knife, cut out stencil. Mark desired placement of stencil design around bottom and neck of sweatshirt.

Lay sweatshirt in single layer on flat surface. Stencil angel design on shirt with white paint and stencil brush, using a dabbing motion. Continue until all cutout areas of stencil are covered. Lift stencil carefully from shirt. Wipe stencil clean of paint before proceeding to next angel. Stencil remaining angels.

Cut a 6" length of ribbon. Tie in a bow and tack to top of angel's dress. Repeat for all angels.

Cross-Stitched Santa Pullover

Materials:
chart on page 149
sweatshirt
6" x 13½" (8.5 count) waste canvas
embroidery flosses (see chart)

Fold the sweatshirt lengthwise to find vertical center. Mark with pins. Pin center of the waste canvas to the mark on the shirt, with top edge of the canvas 4½" from bottom of neckband.

Left: Caroling is even merrier when the carolers are dressed for the season. And unique sweatshirts like these will make everyone feel like singing.

(Make sure canvas is straight.) Baste.

With top line of the design ½" below top edge of canvas, stitch according to chart. Use 6 strands of floss unless otherwise directed.

After stitching, remove canvas according to manufacturer's directions.

Knitted-Yoke Sweatshirt

Materials:
red or green sweatshirt with raglan sleeves
sharp rug needle
1 skein each red and green worsted-weight
  yarn
size 8 (24") circular knitting needle
size 4 (16") circular knitting needle

Note: To decrease, knit 2 stitches together. As the rounds are knitted, compare the knitted yoke to the sweatshirt yoke. If knitted yoke becomes too tight, make fewer decreases.

Draw a line all around the neck of the sweatshirt, 5" from and parallel to the neck opening. Using the rug needle and the yarn for the first stripe, make a running stitch along the line. Space stitches about ¼" apart, making raised ¼" loops on the right side of the sweatshirt. Make a total of 140 loops, evenly spaced around the sweatshirt. Use the size 8 needle to pick up the loops for the first row of knitting around the sweatshirt. Slip a marker on the needle after the last stitch is picked up, to indicate the end of the row.

Working in the round, knit every row and decrease 4 stitches, spaced evenly around the yoke, every other row, beginning with the second row. Work colors in 1" stripes. After the 4th stripe, change to size 4 needle and decrease to 78 stitches. Knit these stitches for 4" to make a rolled collar. Bind off loosely.

Weave in all yarn ends. Cut away sweatshirt yoke about ½" above the first row of knitting. If desired, embellish knitted yoke with bells, bows, or Christmas buttons.

Right: Gold bows and jingle bells glitter on a bright knitted yoke. A joyful jingle will accompany this sweatshirt wherever it goes.

Above: A trio of cross-stitched Santas embellish a plain white pullover.

Above: Stenciled Christmas angels dance on the borders of this country cardigan.

Holiday for the Birds

Carry on a tradition that began hundreds of years ago in Europe: remember the birds at Christmas.

How to make one red flannel cardinal:

Trace bird in photograph (left) to make a pattern for cardinal and wing. (Enlarge pattern on photocopy machine, if desired.) Cut 2 wings and 2 birds from scrap of red flannel, adding ¼″ for seam allowance. Cut one bird from thin batting.

For eye, make a circle with black felt, using small hole punch. Tack circle in place with matching thread. With red embroidery floss, embellish bird's wing and tail as in photograph.

Pin batting to wrong side of bird front. With right sides of bird facing, stitch through all layers, leaving an opening for turning. Turn. With right sides of wings facing, stitch together, leaving an opening for turning. Turn, and slip-stitch openings closed. Stitch front part of finished wing to bird body, leaving wing free in rear.

How to make bread dough wreaths:

Thaw frozen bread dough on a floured surface. Stretch pieces of dough to lengths of approximately 10″. (The elastic dough will try to return to its original shape. If you allow one end of each length to hang over the edge of the counter, its weight will keep it from shrinking.)

Form lengths of dough into wreaths. Braid some of them before forming them into the circular shape. Place them on a greased cookie sheet; allow to rise according to package directions. Bake at recommended temperature until golden brown. Remove from oven and brush tops with beaten egg white. Sprinkle birdseed on top; then bake a few more minutes. Hang wreaths outside with a ribbon or a wire.

How to make decorative birdhouses:

Cut a small block of wood into a house shape, referring to photograph (left) for size and roof angle. Using acrylic paints, try out various painting techniques to achieve a textural look. For chimney, cut one end of a tiny square piece of wood at same angle as roof. Use short piece of dowel for perch. Glue chimney and perch in place, using craft glue.

Below: This double-decker birdhouse sits invitingly in the winter sun. Owner Audrey Julian of Pennsylvania is a collector of handmade birdhouses.

How to make bird snacks:

Use cookie cutters to cut out shapes, pictured above, from bread. Dry shapes in warm oven for 10 minutes. Spread them with peanut butter. Decorate them with seeds, such as niger, sunflower, and millet. Add cranberry halves for a touch of color. For hanging, thread a large darning needle with string and pull it through the top of the "cookie."

For a suet snack, mix suet with birdseed. Press mixture into pinecones. Attach pinecone to a firm branch with florists' wire.

For baskets, cut grapefruit in half. Remove fruit. Punch 4 evenly spaced holes around top of each half. Thread cord through holes for hangers. Fill with mixture of seeds and bits of fruit.

Patterns

Appliquéd Pillows, Wooden House Blocks, and Reindeer Wall Quilt

Instructions are on page 22.
Add ¼″ seam allowance for pillows.
Patterns are full-size.

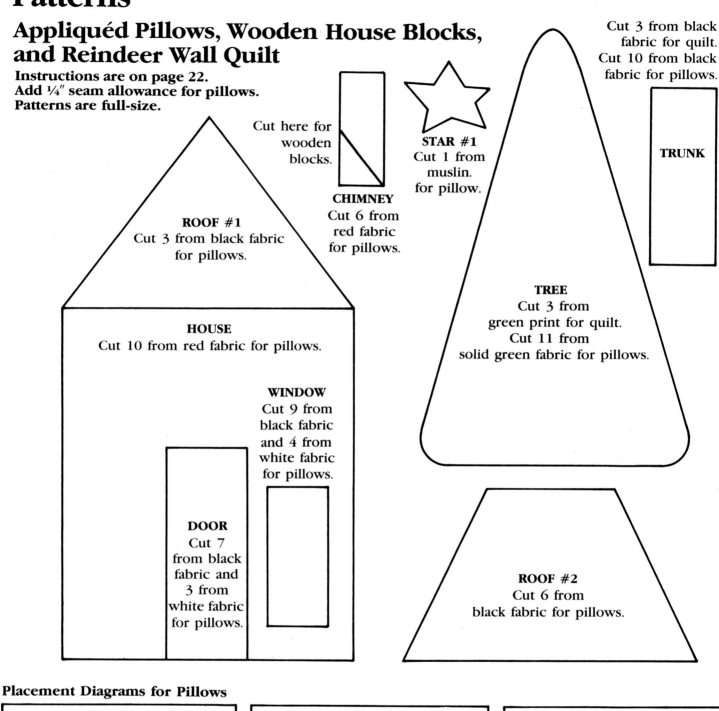

Cut here for wooden blocks.

CHIMNEY
Cut 6 from red fabric for pillows.

STAR #1
Cut 1 from muslin. for pillow.

Cut 3 from black fabric for quilt.
Cut 10 from black fabric for pillows.

TRUNK

ROOF #1
Cut 3 from black fabric for pillows.

HOUSE
Cut 10 from red fabric for pillows.

WINDOW
Cut 9 from black fabric and 4 from white fabric for pillows.

DOOR
Cut 7 from black fabric and 3 from white fabric for pillows.

TREE
Cut 3 from green print for quilt.
Cut 11 from solid green fabric for pillows.

ROOF #2
Cut 6 from black fabric for pillows.

Placement Diagrams for Pillows

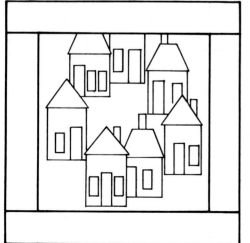

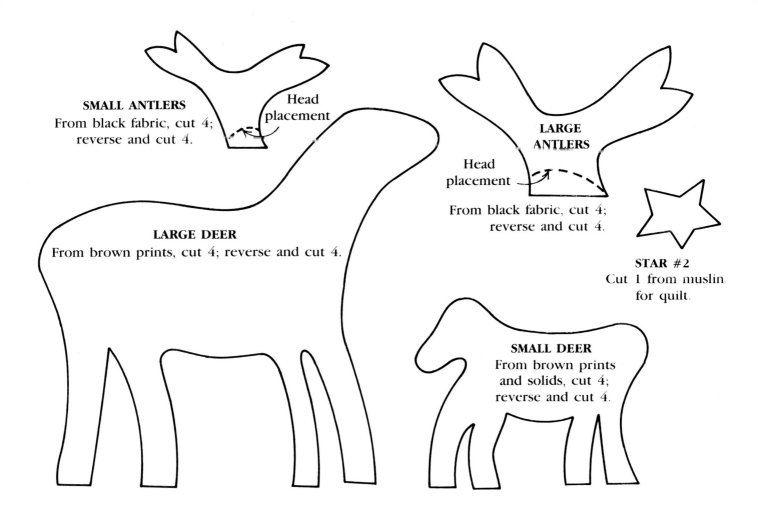

SMALL ANTLERS
From black fabric, cut 4;
reverse and cut 4.

Head
placement

**LARGE
ANTLERS**

Head
placement

From black fabric, cut 4;
reverse and cut 4.

LARGE DEER
From brown prints, cut 4; reverse and cut 4.

STAR #2
Cut 1 from muslin
for quilt.

SMALL DEER
From brown prints
and solids, cut 4;
reverse and cut 4.

Country-Heart Filet Crochet
Instructions are on page 20.

Tea Towel Heart Ornaments
**Instructions are on page 41.
Pattern is full-size.**

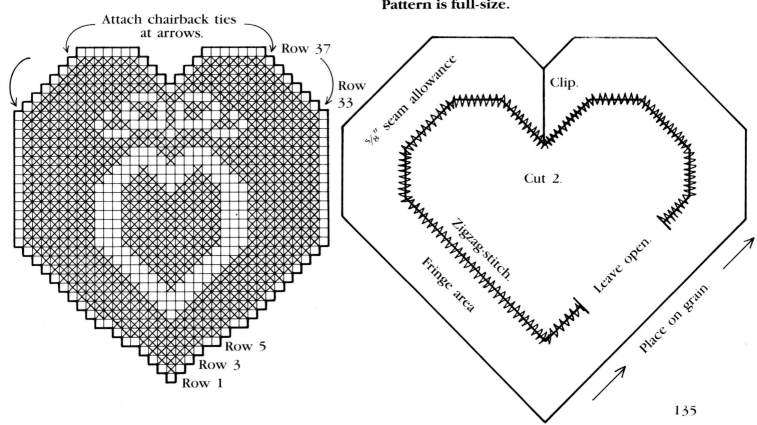

Attach chairback ties
at arrows.

Row 37

Row
33

Row 5
Row 3
Row 1

⅝" seam allowance

Clip.

Cut 2.

Zigzag-stitch

Fringe area

Leave open.

Place on grain.

135

Etched Cake Cover
Instructions are on page 32.

Gift Tags That
Keep on Giving
Instructions are on page 44.

Color Key
(Use 3 strands.)

· DMC 700 Christmas Green
⁄ DMC 666 Christmas Red

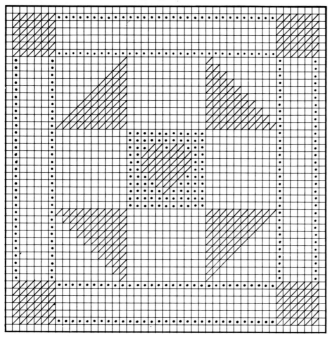

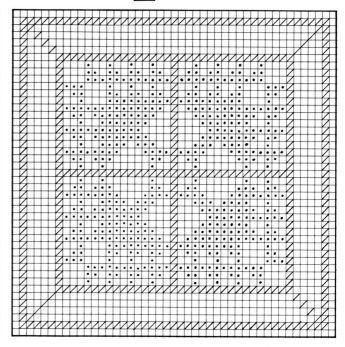

Appliqué a
Country Gift Bag
Instructions are on page 46. Patterns are full-size.

Alphabet Chart for Gift Tags

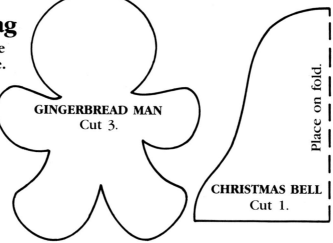

GINGERBREAD MAN
Cut 3.

CHRISTMAS BELL
Cut 1.

Place on fold.

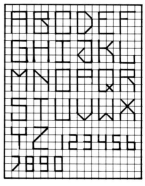

A Calico Bear with Candy Treats
Instructions are on page 49. Pattern is full-size.

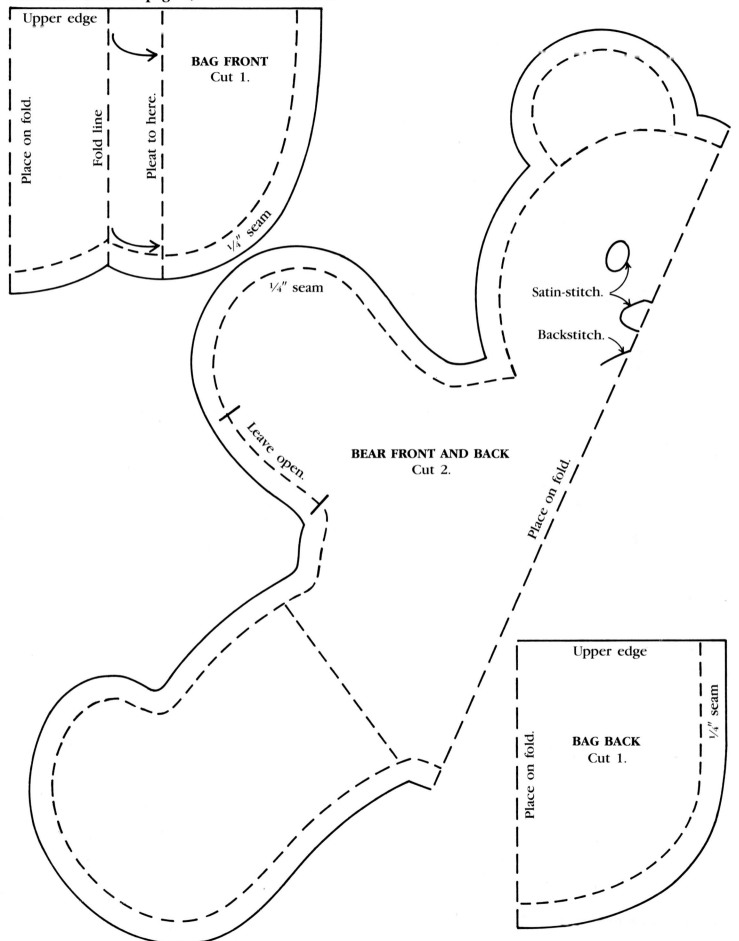

Upper edge

Place on fold.

Fold line

Pleat to here.

BAG FRONT
Cut 1.

¼″ seam

¼″ seam

Satin-stitch.

Backstitch.

Leave open.

BEAR FRONT AND BACK
Cut 2.

Place on fold.

Upper edge

Place on fold.

¼″ seam

BAG BACK
Cut 1.

Christmas Cottage Cookie, Pot Holder, and Ornament

Recipe and instructions are on pages 102 and 103.
Pattern is full-size for pot holder and cookie.
Reduce 50% for ornament.

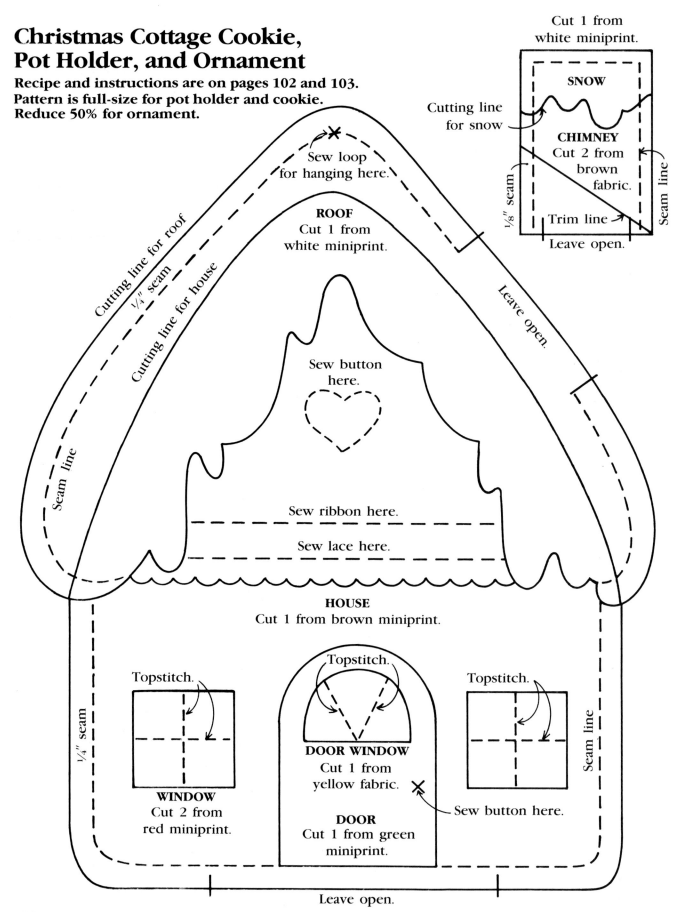

Cut 1 from white miniprint.

SNOW

Cutting line for snow

CHIMNEY
Cut 2 from brown fabric.

1/8" seam

Trim line

Seam line

Leave open.

Cutting line for roof

1/4" seam

Cutting line for house

Seam line

Sew loop for hanging here.

ROOF
Cut 1 from white miniprint.

Leave open.

Sew button here.

Sew ribbon here.

Sew lace here.

HOUSE
Cut 1 from brown miniprint.

Topstitch.

Topstitch.

Topstitch.

1/4" seam

Seam line

WINDOW
Cut 2 from red miniprint.

DOOR WINDOW
Cut 1 from yellow fabric.

Sew button here.

DOOR
Cut 1 from green miniprint.

Leave open.

138

Wood-Burned Gift Basket

**Instructions are on page 51.
Reduce or enlarge patterns
to fit basket.**

Sponge and Spatter These Folk Art Ornaments

Instructions are on page 75. Patterns are full-size.

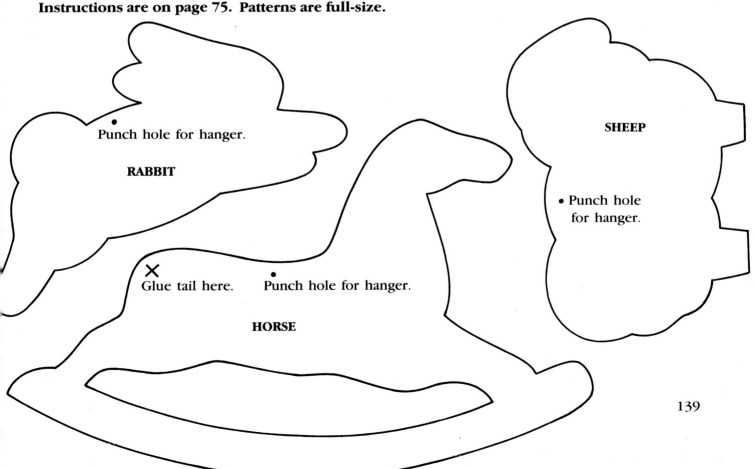

• Punch hole for hanger.

RABBIT

SHEEP

• Punch hole
for hanger.

✕
Glue tail here.   • Punch hole for hanger.

HORSE

Holly Leaf Table Cover

Instructions are on page 61.
Pattern is full-size.
All seam allowances are ¼".

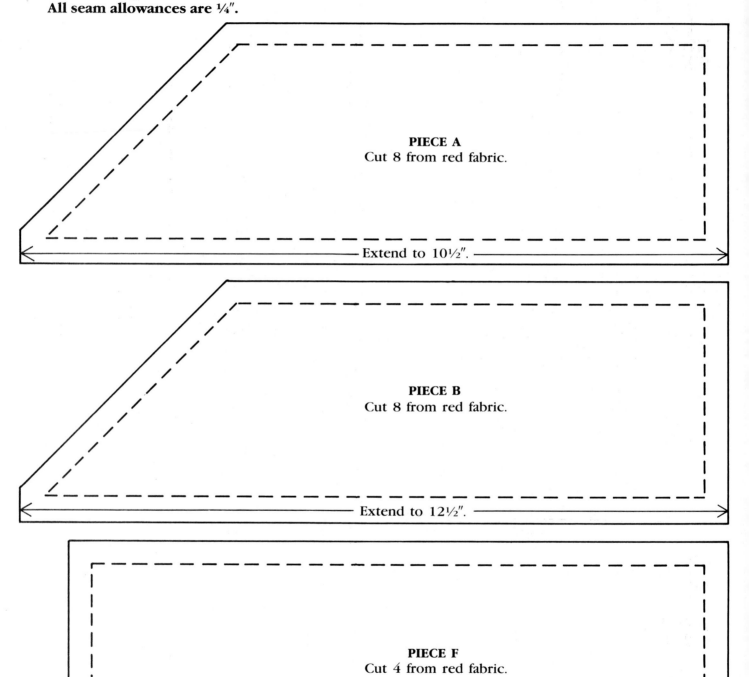

PIECE A
Cut 8 from red fabric.

← Extend to 10½". →

PIECE B
Cut 8 from red fabric.

← Extend to 12½". →

PIECE F
Cut 4 from red fabric.

← Extend to 12½". →

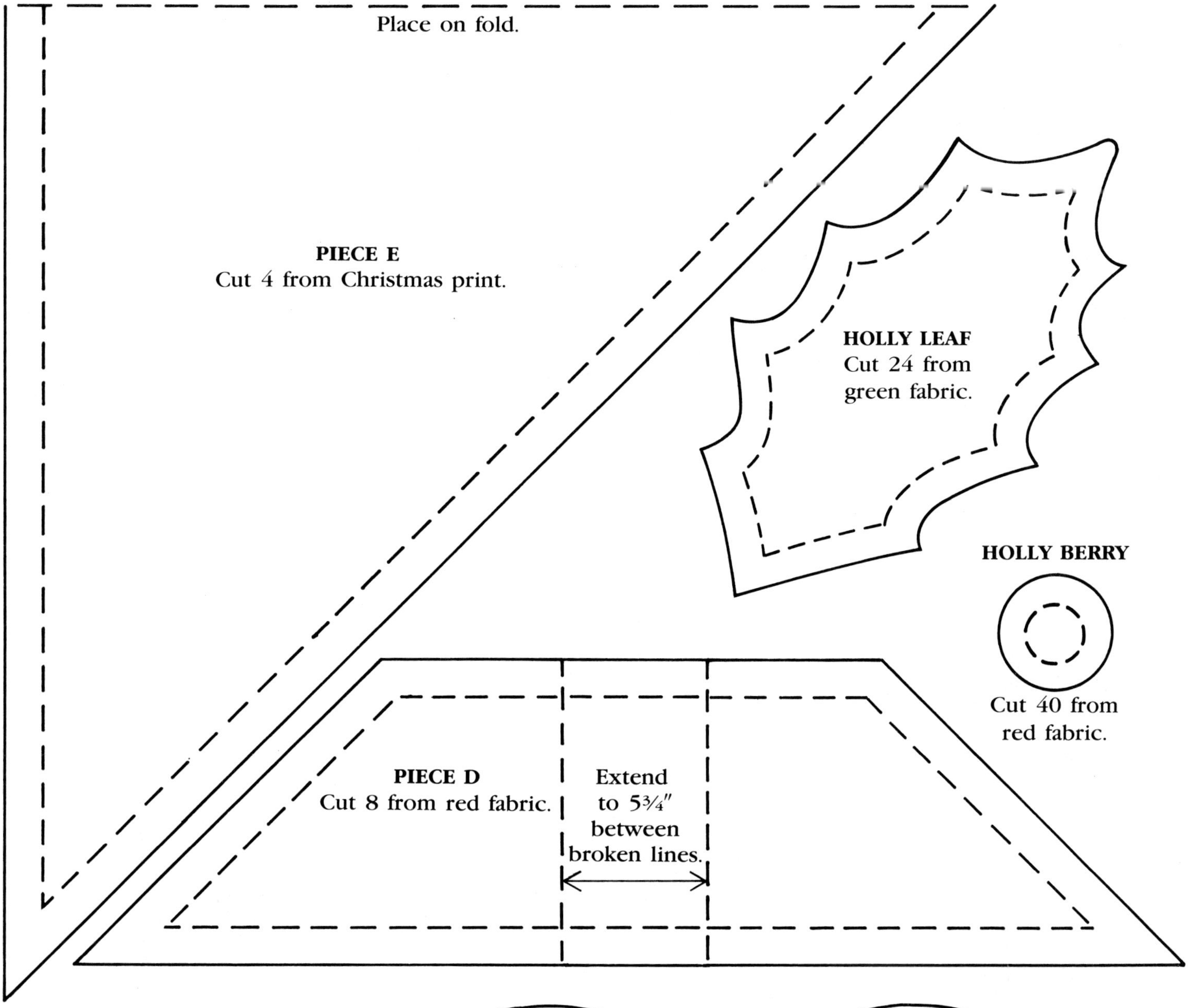

Place on fold.

PIECE E
Cut 4 from Christmas print.

HOLLY LEAF
Cut 24 from
green fabric.

HOLLY BERRY

Cut 40 from
red fabric.

PIECE D
Cut 8 from red fabric.

Extend
to 5¾"
between
broken lines.

Cut 2.

Leave open.

¼" seam

Buffalo Plaid
Napkin Rings

Instructions are on page 74.
Pattern is full-size.

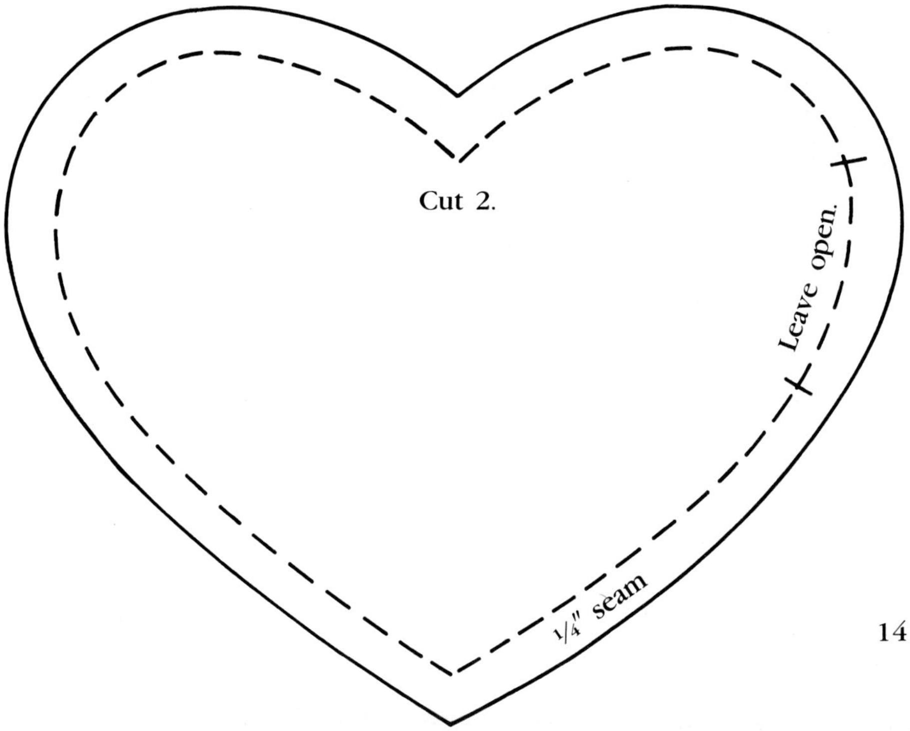

141

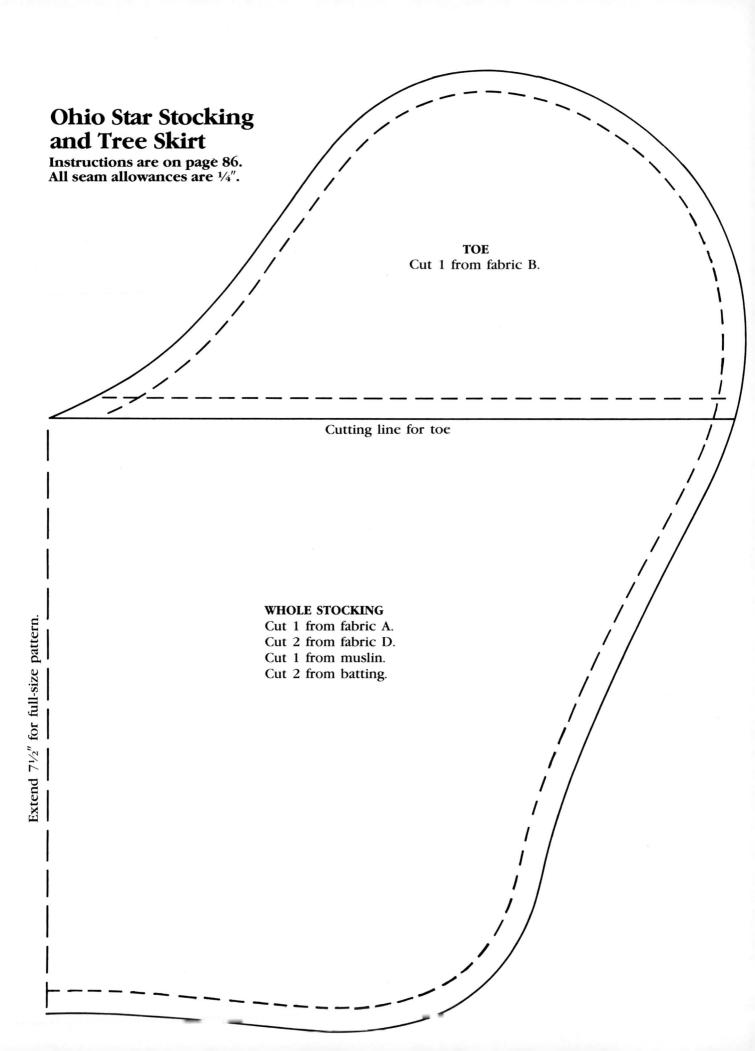

Ohio Star Stocking and Tree Skirt

Instructions are on page 86.
All seam allowances are ¼″.

TOE
Cut 1 from fabric B.

Cutting line for toe

WHOLE STOCKING
Cut 1 from fabric A.
Cut 2 from fabric D.
Cut 1 from muslin.
Cut 2 from batting.

Extend 7½″ for full-size pattern.

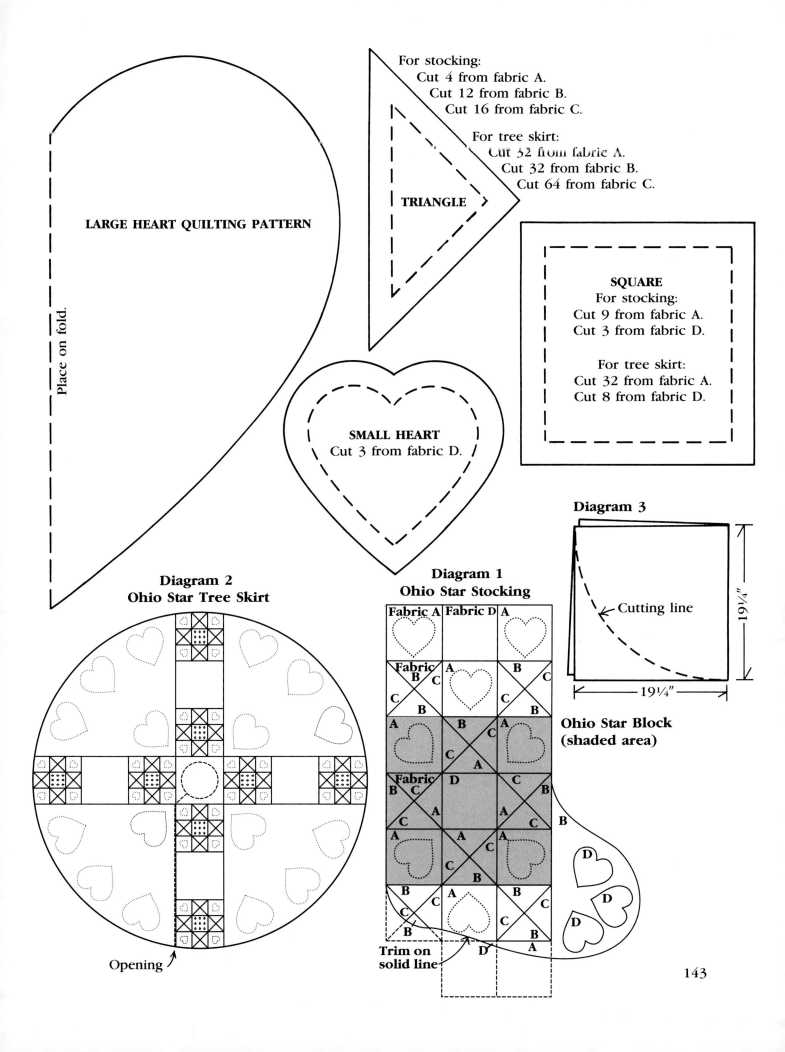

LARGE HEART QUILTING PATTERN

Place on fold.

TRIANGLE

For stocking:
Cut 4 from fabric A.
Cut 12 from fabric B.
Cut 16 from fabric C.

For tree skirt:
Cut 32 from fabric A.
Cut 32 from fabric B.
Cut 64 from fabric C.

SQUARE
For stocking:
Cut 9 from fabric A.
Cut 3 from fabric D.

For tree skirt:
Cut 32 from fabric A.
Cut 8 from fabric D.

SMALL HEART
Cut 3 from fabric D.

Diagram 3

Cutting line

19¼"

19¼"

Diagram 2
Ohio Star Tree Skirt

Opening

Diagram 1
Ohio Star Stocking

Fabric A	Fabric D	A

Fabric
B
C
A
B
C

A
B
A
C

Fabric
B
C
D
C
A
C
B

A
A
A
C
B

B
C
A
B
C
A

Trim on
solid line

D

**Ohio Star Block
(shaded area)**

D
D
D

143

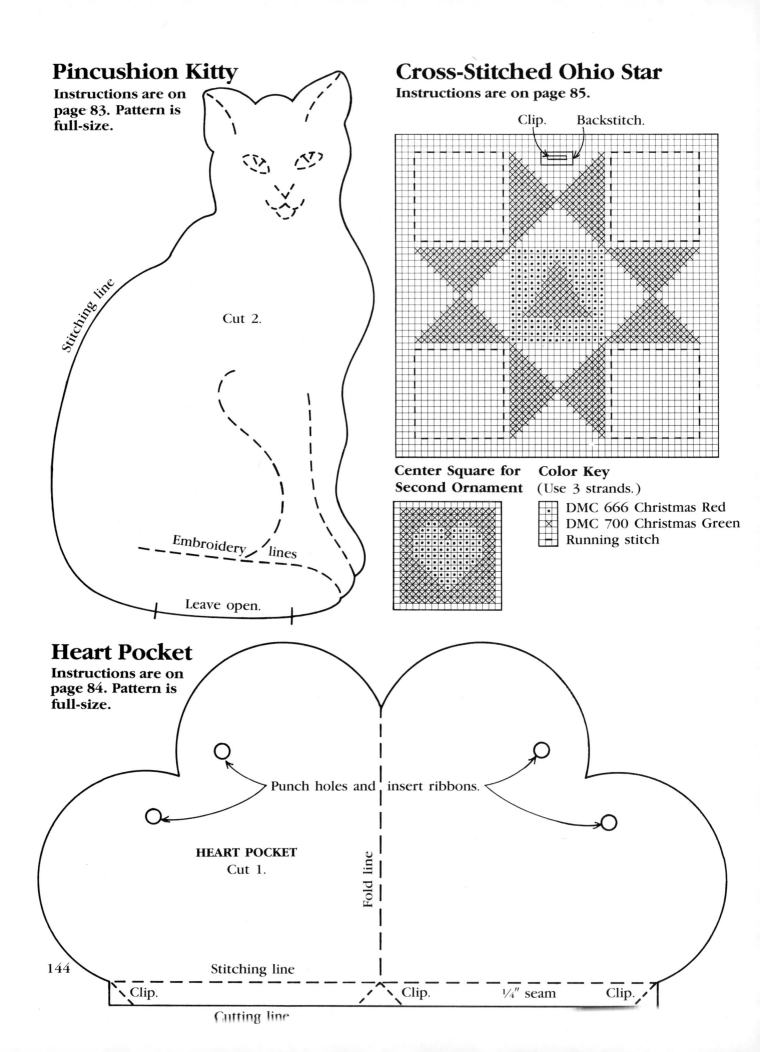

Pincushion Kitty

Instructions are on page 83. Pattern is full-size.

Stitching line

Cut 2.

Embroidery lines

Leave open.

Cross-Stitched Ohio Star

Instructions are on page 85.

Clip.   Backstitch.

Center Square for Second Ornament

Color Key
(Use 3 strands.)

⊡	DMC 666 Christmas Red
✕	DMC 700 Christmas Green
☐	Running stitch

Heart Pocket

Instructions are on page 84. Pattern is full-size.

Punch holes and insert ribbons.

HEART POCKET
Cut 1.

Fold line

144

Stitching line

Clip.   Clip.   ¼" seam   Clip.

Cutting line

Bitty Bears

Instructions are on page 82.
Pattern is full-size and includes ¼″ seam allowance. Cut foot and paw pads from suede or felt. Cut all other pieces from woven fabric.

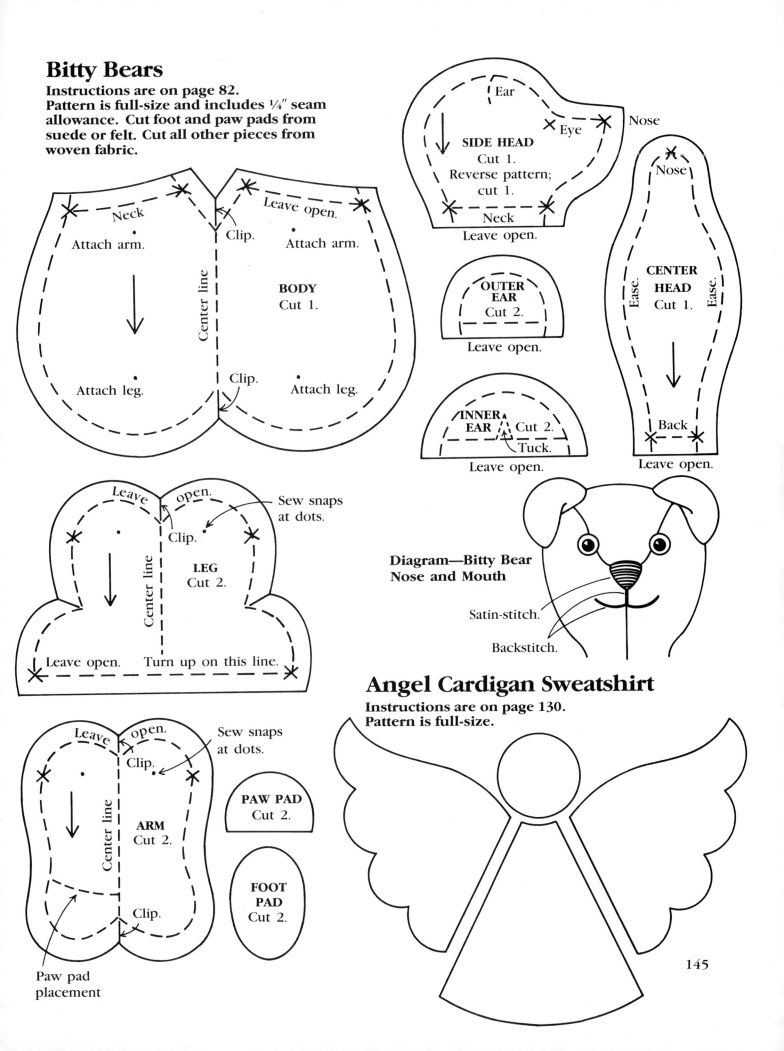

Ear

Eye

Nose

SIDE HEAD
Cut 1.
Reverse pattern;
cut 1.

Neck

Leave open.

Nose

CENTER HEAD
Cut 1.

Ease.

Ease.

Back

Leave open.

OUTER EAR
Cut 2.

Leave open.

INNER EAR Cut 2.

Tuck.

Leave open.

Neck

Attach arm.

Leave open.

Clip.

Attach arm.

Center line

BODY
Cut 1.

Attach leg.

Clip.

Attach leg.

Leave open.

Clip.

Sew snaps at dots.

Center line

LEG
Cut 2.

Leave open. Turn up on this line.

Diagram—Bitty Bear Nose and Mouth

Satin-stitch.

Backstitch.

Leave open.

Clip.

Sew snaps at dots.

Center line

ARM
Cut 2.

Clip.

Paw pad placement

PAW PAD
Cut 2.

FOOT PAD
Cut 2.

Angel Cardigan Sweatshirt

Instructions are on page 130.
Pattern is full-size.

145

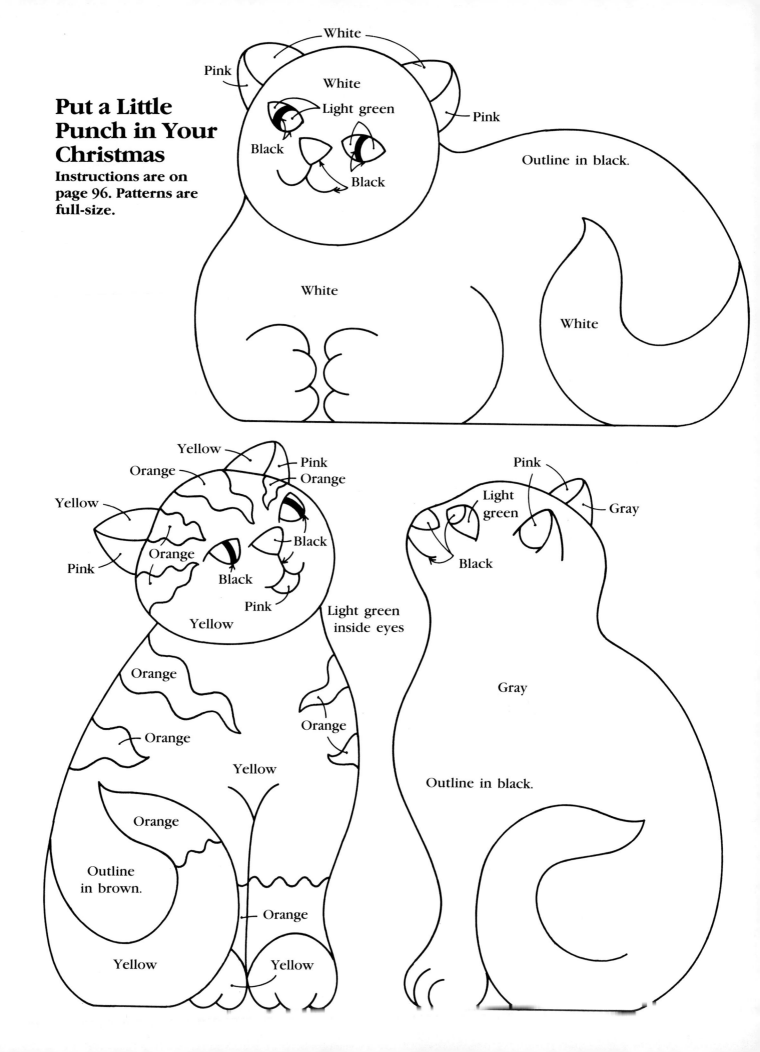

Put a Little Punch in Your Christmas

Instructions are on page 96. Patterns are full-size.

White

Pink

White

Light green

Black

Black

Pink

Outline in black.

White

White

Yellow

Orange

Pink
Orange

Yellow

Yellow

Orange

Pink

Black

Orange

Black

Pink

Yellow

Light green
inside eyes

Orange

Orange

Orange

Yellow

Orange

Outline
in brown.

Orange

Yellow

Yellow

Pink

Light
green

Gray

Black

Gray

Outline in black.

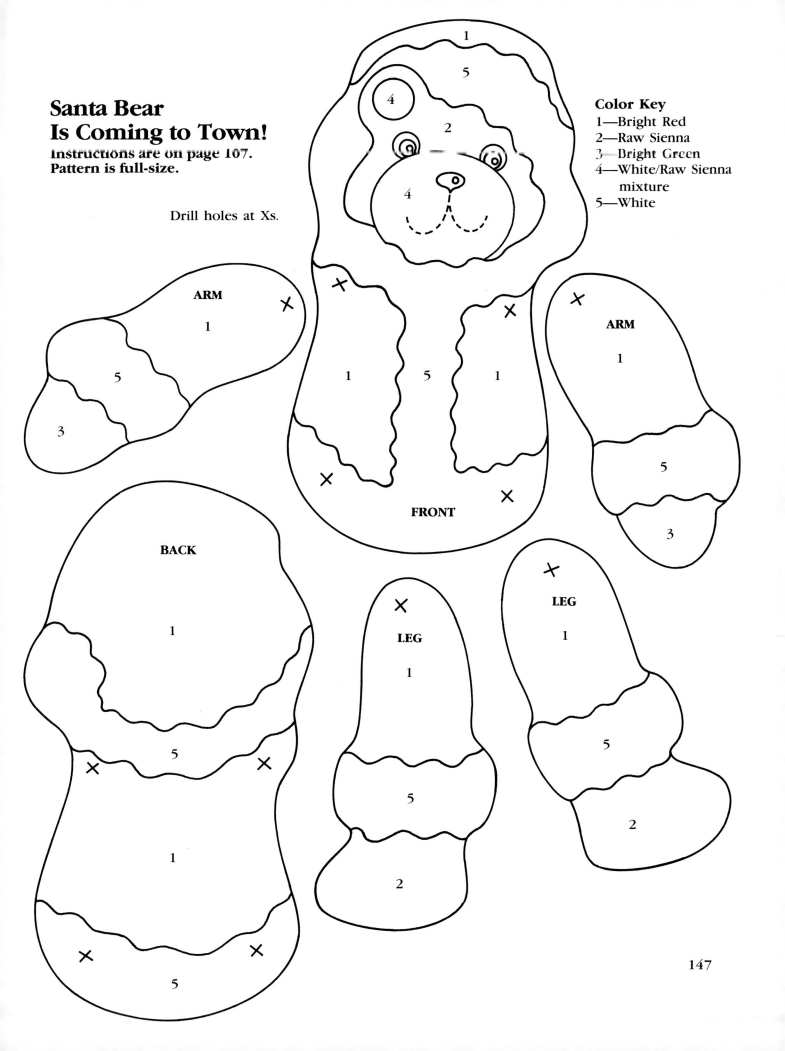

Santa Bear
Is Coming to Town!

Instructions are on page 107.
Pattern is full-size.

Drill holes at Xs.

Color Key
1—Bright Red
2—Raw Sienna
3—Bright Green
4—White/Raw Sienna
   mixture
5—White

ARM
1
5
3

ARM
1
5
3

FRONT
1
5
1
5
1

BACK
1
5
1
5

LEG
1
5
2

LEG
1
5
2

147

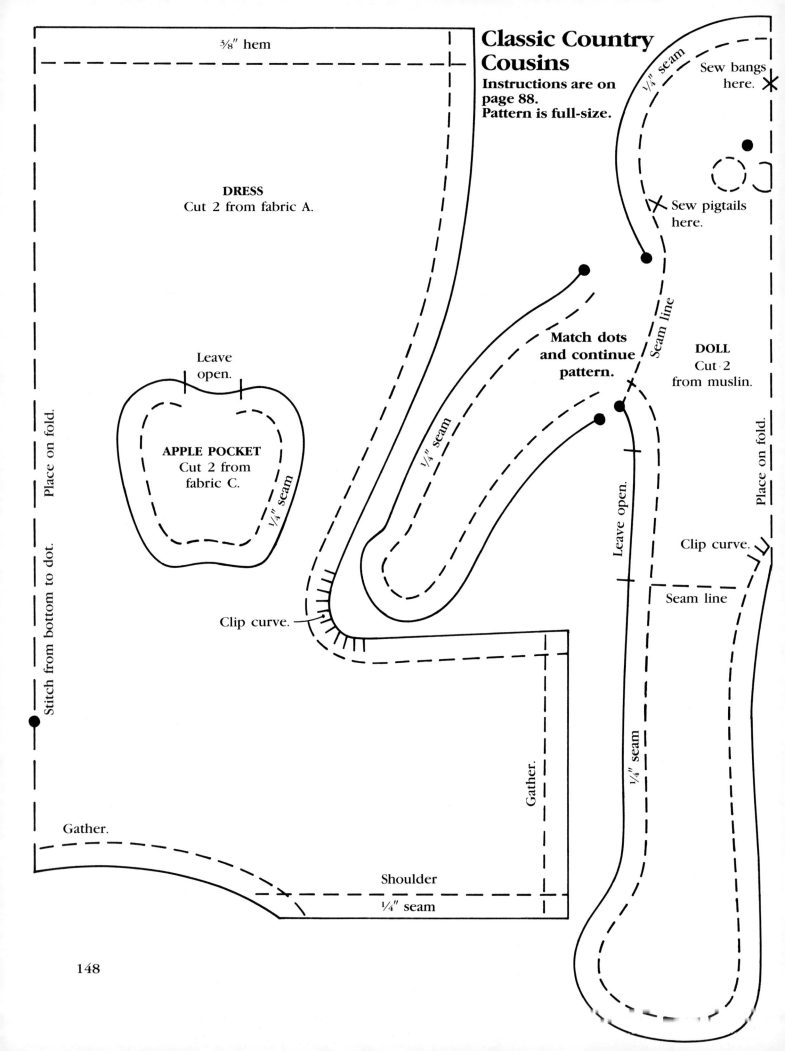

⅜" hem

Classic Country Cousins
Instructions are on page 88.
Pattern is full-size.

¼" seam

Sew bangs here. ✕

Sew pigtails here. ✕

Seam line

DRESS
Cut 2 from fabric A.

Leave open.

Match dots and continue pattern.

DOLL
Cut 2 from muslin.

Place on fold

APPLE POCKET
Cut 2 from fabric C.

¼" seam

¼" seam

Stitch from bottom to dot.

Place on fold

Leave open.

Clip curve.

Seam line

Clip curve.

Gather.

¼" seam

Gather.

Shoulder

¼" seam

148

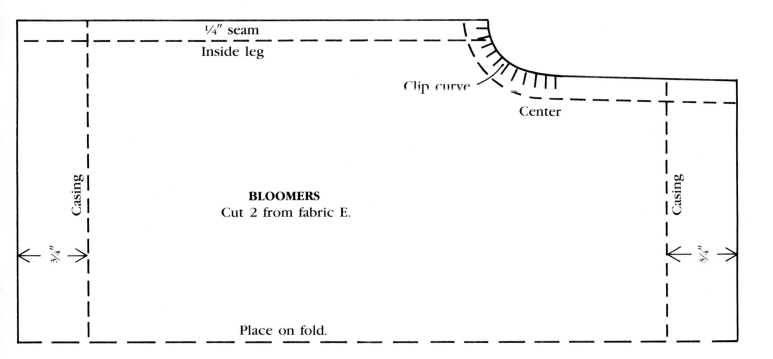

¼″ seam

Inside leg

Clip curve

Center

Casing

BLOOMERS
Cut 2 from fabric E.

Casing

¾″

¾″

Place on fold.

Cross-Stitched Santa Pullover
Instructions are on page 130.

Color Key
(Use 6 strands.)

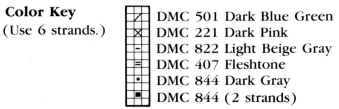

DMC 501 Dark Blue Green
DMC 221 Dark Pink
DMC 822 Light Beige Gray
DMC 407 Fleshtone
DMC 844 Dark Gray
DMC 844 (2 strands)

149

i love
Christmas!

BIB
Cut 1 from red-on-white pindot.

A Christmas Teddy Sweatshirt

**Instructions are on page 128.
Pattern is full-size.**

NOSE
Cut 1 from
brown felt.

CHEEK
Cut 2 from
red calico.

¼" seam

Paddy placement

PADDY
Cut 6 from
light brown
pindot.

PAW PAD
Cut 2 from
light brown
pindot.

Paw pad
placement

Satin-stitch.

BEAR BODY
Cut 2 from medium
brown pindot.
Cut 1 from fleece.

Cheek
placement

Bib placement

Muzzle placement

Nose
placement

Satin-stitch.

Place on fold.

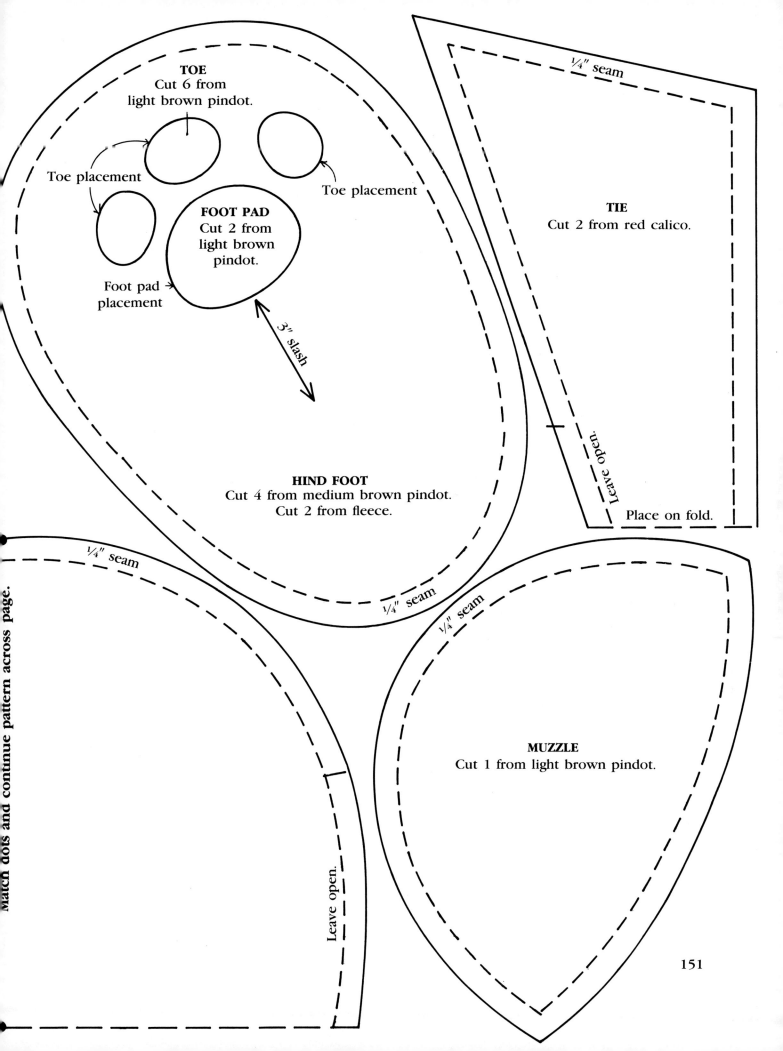

TOE
Cut 6 from
light brown pindot.

Toe placement

Toe placement

FOOT PAD
Cut 2 from
light brown
pindot.

Foot pad
placement

3" slash

HIND FOOT
Cut 4 from medium brown pindot.
Cut 2 from fleece.

¼" seam

¼" seam

¼" seam

TIE
Cut 2 from red calico.

Leave open.

Place on fold.

¼" seam

¼" seam

MUZZLE
Cut 1 from light brown pindot.

Leave open.

Match dots and continue pattern across page.

151

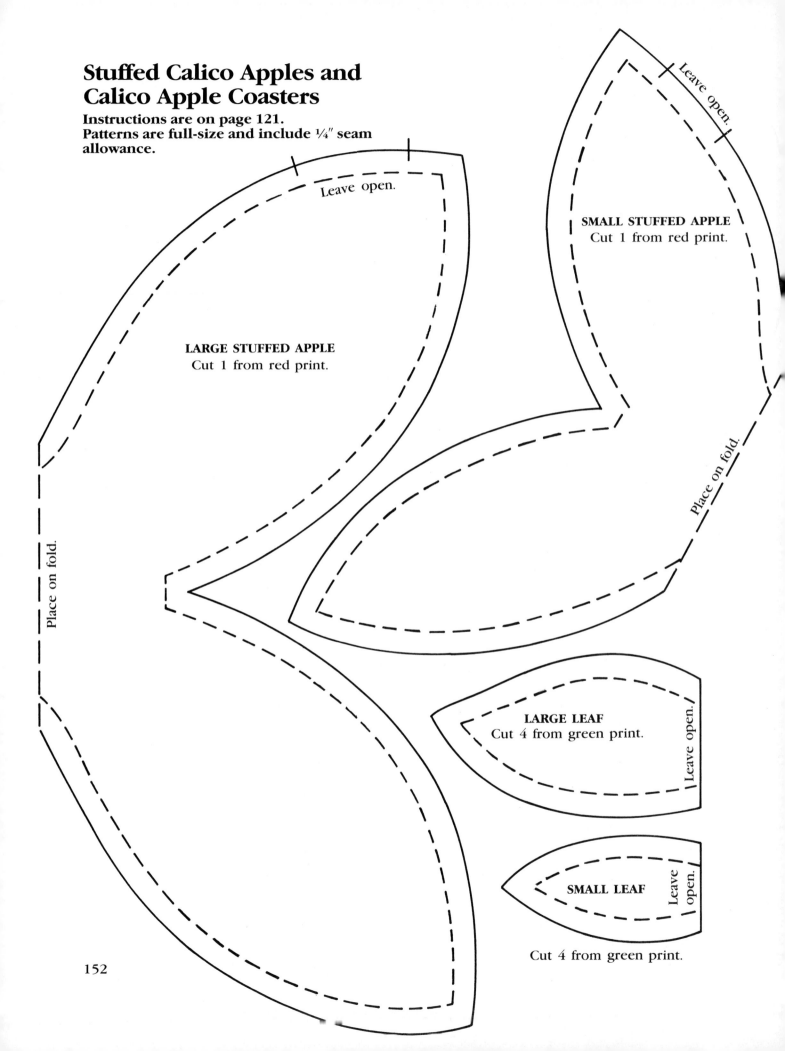

Stuffed Calico Apples and Calico Apple Coasters

Instructions are on page 121.
Patterns are full-size and include ¼″ seam allowance.

Leave open.

LARGE STUFFED APPLE
Cut 1 from red print.

Place on fold.

Leave open.

SMALL STUFFED APPLE
Cut 1 from red print.

Place on fold.

LARGE LEAF
Cut 4 from green print.

Leave open.

SMALL LEAF
Leave open.

Cut 4 from green print.

152

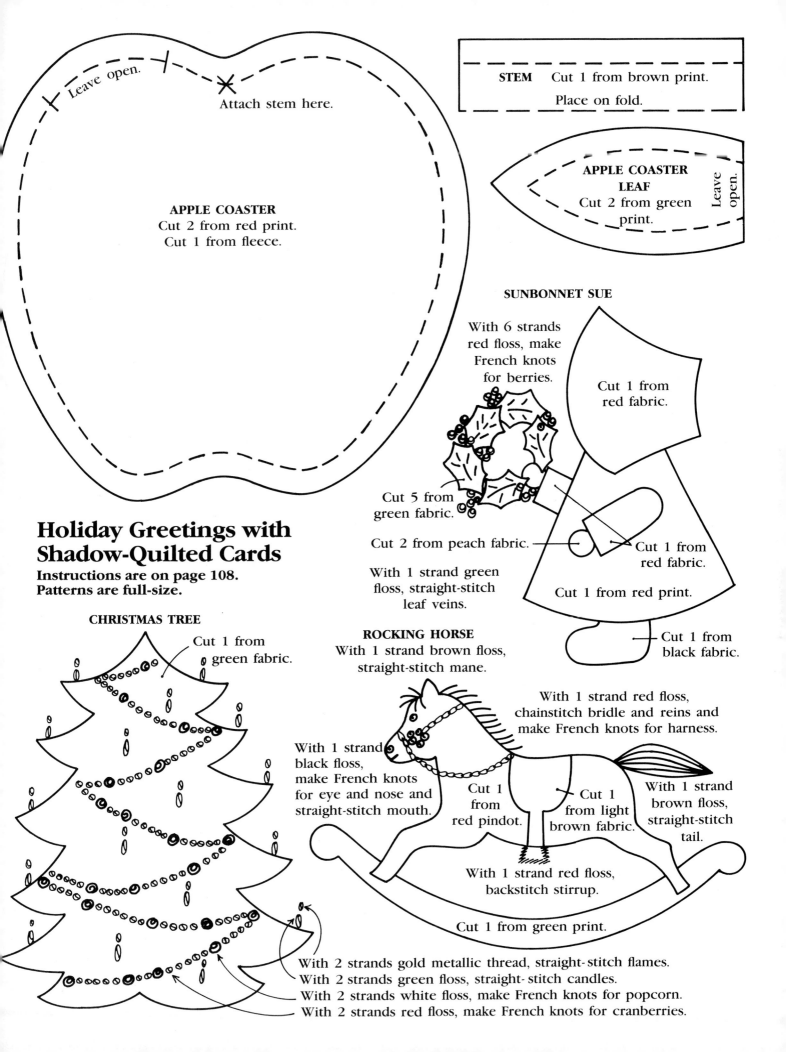

Leave open.

✂ **Attach stem here.**

STEM Cut 1 from brown print.
Place on fold.

APPLE COASTER LEAF
Cut 2 from green print.

Leave open.

APPLE COASTER
Cut 2 from red print.
Cut 1 from fleece.

SUNBONNET SUE

With 6 strands red floss, make French knots for berries.

Cut 1 from red fabric.

Cut 5 from green fabric.

Cut 2 from peach fabric.

With 1 strand green floss, straight-stitch leaf veins.

Cut 1 from red fabric.

Cut 1 from red print.

Cut 1 from black fabric.

Holiday Greetings with Shadow-Quilted Cards
**Instructions are on page 108.
Patterns are full-size.**

CHRISTMAS TREE

Cut 1 from green fabric.

ROCKING HORSE
With 1 strand brown floss, straight-stitch mane.

With 1 strand red floss, chainstitch bridle and reins and make French knots for harness.

With 1 strand black floss, make French knots for eye and nose and straight-stitch mouth.

Cut 1 from red pindot.

Cut 1 from light brown fabric.

With 1 strand brown floss, straight-stitch tail.

With 1 strand red floss, backstitch stirrup.

Cut 1 from green print.

With 2 strands gold metallic thread, straight-stitch flames.
With 2 strands green floss, straight-stitch candles.
With 2 strands white floss, make French knots for popcorn.
With 2 strands red floss, make French knots for cranberries.

Contributors

Designers

Janice Ford Bills, Santa letter ornaments, 129.

Linda R. Brandt, folk art ornaments, 75.

Joanne Burkhart, country cousins, 89; apples, coasters, 122.

Patricia Ramey Channell, calico bear, 48; cat ornaments, 95; cardigan, 130.

Bea Crowell, gift tags, 42; cross-stitched ornaments, 83.

Susan Z. Douglas, knitted sheep, 106.

Zelda W. Fasciano, shadow-quilted cards, 109.

Connie Formby, food wraps, 50, lower left 51.

Dot Formby, cardinals, bird wreaths, 132.

Joyce M. Gillis, teddy bear sweatshirt, 128.

Barb Griffin, appliquéd bags, 45; pot holder and ornament, 103.

Memory E. Hagler, knitted sweatshirt yoke, 130.

Charlotte Hagood, crazy-quilt fan, 79; coverlet ornaments, 66; button wreath, pincushion kitty, heart pocket, button man, shell pincushion, 83; cookie-mold ornaments, 104.

Janet Harlow, tea towel hearts, 40.

Jellicle Original, *putz* sheep, 63.

Lynn Langworthy, stocking and tree skirt, 86–87.

Barbara LeQuire, bitty bears, 82.

Lauré Parish, Santa bear, 107.

Lamon Roy, crafting of walnut baskets, 39.

Eunice Svinicki, crocheted chair backs and place mats, 20.

Carol M. Tipton, wooden house blocks adaptation, 23; spoon tree, 41; wood-burning for market basket, 51; napkin rings, 73; button brooch, 78.

Joan Vibert, appliquéd pillows, house blocks design, 23; quilt, 24; Santa sweatshirt, 130.

Carol L. Wagner, table cover, 61.

Julie A. Wilson, paper stars, 68.

Photographers

Gary Clark, 30–31, 39, 41, 54–55, lower right 56, 76–77, 82, 106, 107, 123.

Colleen Duffley, senior photographer, cover, 2–3, right 10, 17, 20–21, 24–29, 33, 34, 37, 38, 42, 45, 47, 48, 50, lower left 51, 52–53, 59, 61, 63, 68–69, 73, 75, 78–79, 80–81, 89, 97–99, 101–103, l04–l05, 109, 112–113, 119, 122, 125, 128–132, upper left 133.

Tom Hendrickson, 35.

Mary-Gray Hunter, left 10, 23, upper left 51, 83, 85–87, 95.

Hal Lott, 4–9.

Sylvia Martin, 90–94.

Beth Maynor, 12–15, lower left and upper 56, 64–65, 114–117, lower right 133.

John O'Hagan, 11, 40, left 54, 57, 66, 70–71.

Cheryl Sales, 110–111.

Melissa Springer, upper right 133.

Photostylists

Kay Clarke, 17, 20–21, 33, 34, 37, 38, 42, 45, 48, 59, 73, 97–99, 101–103, 119, 122, 125, 128.

Connie Formby, 10, 50, lower left 51, upper right 133.

Joetta Moulden, 4–9.

Acknowledgments:

Photo on page 89 was shot at Looney House, Ashville, Alabama.

Snowshoes on page 73 provided courtesy of L.L. Bean, Freeport, Maine.

Special thanks to:
Kathleen English
Margaret Allen Northen

Sources:

To order ceramic cookie molds used on page 104, contact Brown Bag Cookie Art, Box F, Hill, NH 03243.

For Christmas prints (used on page 51), request the *Complete Pictorial Archive Catalog* from Dover Publications, Inc., 31 East 2nd Street, Mineola, NY 11501.

To order a precut rose stencil used on page 32, contact Eastern Craft Supply, P.O. Box 341, Dept. 26000, Wyckoff, NJ 07481.

To order the book mentioned on page 77, send $5 and your name and address to *Treasures of the Heart and Hand*, Route 4, Box 520, Lenoir City, TN 37771.

For details on Noah's arks (see page 54), write to Sherry Phillips, 5328 Hickory Hollow Road, Knoxville, TN 37919.

For a catalog of overshot place mats (used on page 67), write to The Chamomile Shop, P.O. Box 619, Rangeley, ME 04970.

To order a fresh-cut fraser fir (seen on page 83), write to Laurel Springs Fraser Firs, P.O. Box 85, Laurel Springs, NC 28644.

For information about the Silver Leaf Country Inn (see page 123), contact Norma Crow, Route 1, Box 122, Lyles, TN 37098.

Index

General

Antique button brooch, 78
Appliqué
  bear sweatshirt, 128
  Christmas cottage
    ornament and pot
    holder, 103
  gift bags, 45
  pillows, 22
  reindeer wall quilt, 24
  cards, 108
Apron, stenciled, 47
Aromatic simmer, 38

Beeswax ornaments, 67,
  85
Birdhouses, 132
Bird snacks, 132–133
Button craft
  brooch, 78
  button man, 84
  crazy-quilt fan, 79
  wreath, 83

Cards, shadow-quilted,
  108
Collectibles
  Noah's arks, 54–57
  Santas, 114–117
  sewing notions, 83
  tea sets, 40
Country dolls, 88
Country inn, 123
Country sheep, 106
Crochet
  chair backs, 17, 20
  place mats, 17, 20
Cross-stitch
  gift tags, 42, 44
  ornaments, 85
  Santa sweatshirt, 130

Decorating
  miniwreaths, 28
  Moravian *putz*, 64
  New England
    saltbox-style home,
    4–9
  Santa Fe wreaths,
    25–27
  with grapevines, 10
  with handiwork,
    90–94
  with herbs, 12–15
  with Noah's arks,
    54–57
  with Santa collection,
    57, 114–117
Dolls, country, 88

Embroidery
  cards, 108
  crazy-quilt fan
    ornament, 79
  punch needle, 95
Etched cake cover,
  32–34

Folk art
  Moravian *putz,* 64–65
  Noah's arks, 54–57, 93
  Santas, 57, 114–117
Friendship apron, 47

Gift wrap and packaging
  appliquéd gift bags, 45
  bottle wraps, 50
  citrus garlands, 37
  cross-stitched gift tags,
    42, 44
  food wraps, 50
  jar toppers, 37, 42
  muslin gift bags, 77
  paper doilies, 50
  paper gift bags, 51, 77

  stenciled wraps, 23
  wood-burned baskets,
    51
Gingerbread houses, 35
Grapevines, 10

Heart pocket, 84
Herbs, 12–15
Holly leaf table cover,
  61

Inn, country, 123

Knitting
  country sheep, 106
  sweatshirt yoke, 131

Napkin rings, 74
Needlecrafter's tree,
  83–85

Ornaments
  baker's tree, 39
  beeswax, 67, 85
  birdseed snacks, 133
  button man, 84
  button wreath, 83
  cardinal, red flannel,
    132
  Christmas cottage,
    103
  colonial coverlet, 67
  cookie cutters, 39, 41
  cookie-mold, 104–105
  cookies, 41, 101
  crazy-quilt fan, 79
  cross-stitched Ohio
    Star, 85
  embroidery floss
    garland, 83
  heart pocket, 84

  letters to Santa, 129
  paper chains, 66, 110
  paper doll garlands,
    110
  paper lanterns, 110
  paper spirals, 110
  pincushion kitty, 83
  pom-pom, 94
  punch-embroidered
    cats, 95–96
  putz sheep, 63
  sewing notions, 83
  shell pincushion, 85
  snowflakes, 110
  spice, 14–15
  sponge- and
    spatter-painted
    animals, 75
  stars, folded paper, 68
  stars, sweet gum, 67
  tea towel hearts, 41
  tea tree, 40
  wallpaper scrap, 94
  walnut baskets, 39
  wooden birdhouses,
    132
  wreaths, bread dough,
    132

Paper
  chains, 66, 110
  confetti, 110
  cookie-mold
    ornaments, 104
  lanterns, 110
  paper doll garlands,
    110
  paper stars, 66, 68
  snowflakes, 110
  spirals, 110
Pillows
  appliquéd pillows,
    22–23
  country sheep, 106
Place mats, 17, 20

Pot holder, 103
Punch-embroidered cats, 95
Putz, 64

Quilting
  cards, 108
  holly leaf table cover, 61
  Ohio Star stocking and tree skirt, 86–87

Santa
  bear, wooden toy, 107
  collection, 114–117
  letter ornaments, 129
Sheep
  knitted, 106
  molded, 63
Shell pincushion, 85
Stars
  paper, two-color, 68
  sweet gum, 67
Stenciling
  friendship apron, 47
  gift wrap, 23
  sweatshirt, 130
Stocking, Ohio Star, 86
Stuffed calico apples, 121
Sweatshirts
  angel cardigan, 130
  knitted yoke, 131
  Santa pullover, 130
  teddy bear, 128

Table dressings
  napkin rings, 74
  country-heart place mats, 17, 20
  holly leaf table cover, 61–62
Toys and stuffed animals
  bitty bears, 82
  country dolls, 88
  country sheep, 106
  Santa bear wooden toy, 107
Tree skirt, Ohio Star, 86–87

Trees
  baker's, 39
  cotton-wrapped, 92
  feather, 93
  grapevine, 10–11
  needlecrafter's, 83–85
  Noah's ark, 56
  pinecone, 4
  spoon, 41
  star, 66–69
  tabletops, 39–41
  tea, 40

Walnut baskets, 39
Wood
  birdhouses, 132
  house blocks, 22
  letters to Santa, 129
  Santa bear toy, 107
  spoon tree, 41
Wreaths
  bread dough, 132
  button, 83
  cat, 14
  gingerroot, 38
  miniwreaths, 28–29
  Santa, 12
  Santa Fe, 25–27

Recipes

Apples, baked, with custard sauce, 121

Banana-peanut loaves, 125
Beef stew en croûte, 120
Beverages
  cherry drink, 125
  fruit juice drink, 74
  fruit nog, spiced, 118
  mocha mix, 44
  wassail, 120
Brandied fruit, 36
Breads
  banana-peanut loaves, 125

bread wreaths, savory pepper, 19
coffee cake crown, Saint Lucia's, 61
houska, 60
muffins, orange-raisin bran, 124
panettone, 60
yuletide rounds, 58
Buckwheat flapjacks with blueberry-lemon syrup, 72

Cakes
  applesauce mini-fruitcakes, 34
  chocolate-cherry cola cake, 32
Candies
  Christmas tree bark, 49
  malted-sugar taffy, 49
  marzipan, 127
Cole slaw, cabbage patch, 120
Cookies
  chocolate-peanut butter basket-weave, 97
  Christmas cottage stenciled, 102
  cookie party pizzas, 126
  quilted spice, 100
  redware pumpkin, 100
  stained-glass candy, 101
  thimble, 101
  toasted oatmeal lace, 102
Cornish hens, currant-glazed, 16

Desserts
  apples, baked, with custard sauce, 121
  cake, chocolate-cherry cola, 32
  fruitcakes, 34
  pastry squares, vanilla crème, 19

sundae sandwiches, brownie-mint, 126

Gifts, food
  bean soup mix, 44
  brandied fruit, 36
  Christmas jam, 43
  herbal honey, 38
  mocha mix, 44
  olive oil, garlic-flavored, 36
  pecans, toasted, 43
  peppers, roasted, 36
  pickled pineapple, 43
  snack mix, travelers', 36
  wine vinegar, 38

Muffins, orange-raisin bran, 124

Salmon omelets, 74
Salad, vinaigrette, 18
Sauces, syrups, and toppings
  blueberry-lemon syrup, 72
  brandied fruit, 36
  custard sauce, 121
  herbal honey sauce, 38
  mint-fudge sauce, 126
Soups and stews
  bean soup, 44
  beef stew en croûte, 120

Vegetables
  casserole, potato-green bean, 118
  coleslaw, cabbage patch, 120
  sweet potatoes and oranges, 18
  timbales, brussels sprouts-Swiss cheese, 18
  wild rice combo, 16